Contents

Chapter 1: Privacy

Chapter 2: Online Safety

Chapter 3: Do We Really Have Privacy?

Introduction

Protecting Our Privacy is volume 451 in the **issues** series. The aim of the series is to offer current, diverse information about important issues in our world, from a UK perspective.

About *Protecting our Privacy*

Privacy in an online world is becoming increasingly difficult. Everything you do online is recorded, leaving a digital shadow behind you. This book looks at ways to protect your data, spot scams, and staying safe online.

Our sources

Titles in the **issues** series are designed to function as educational resource books, providing a balanced overview of a specific subject.

The information in our books is comprised of facts, articles and opinions from many different sources, including:

- Newspaper reports and opinion pieces
- Website factsheets
- Magazine and journal articles
- Statistics and surveys
- Government reports
- Literature from special interest groups.

A note on critical evaluation

Because the information reprinted here is from a number of different sources, readers should bear in mind the origin of the text and whether the source is likely to have a particular bias when presenting information (or when conducting their research). It is hoped that, as you read about the many aspects of the issues explored in this book, you will critically evaluate the information presented.

It is important that you decide whether you are being presented with facts or opinions. Does the writer give a biased or unbiased report? If an opinion is being expressed, do you agree with the writer? Is there potential bias to the 'facts' or statistics behind an article?

Activities

Throughout this book, you will find a selection of assignments and activities designed to help you engage with the articles you have been reading and to explore your own opinions. Some tasks will take longer than others and there is a mixture of design, writing and research-based activities that you can complete alone or in a group.

Further research

At the end of each article we have listed its source and a website that you can visit if you would like to conduct your own research. Please remember to critically evaluate any sources that you consult and consider whether the information you are viewing is accurate and unbiased.

Issues Online

The **issues** series of books is complemented by our online resource, issuesonline.co.uk

On the Issues Online website you will find a wealth of information, covering over 75 topics, to support the PSHE and RSE curriculum.

Why Issues Online?

Researching a topic? Issues Online is the best place to start for...

Librarians

Issues Online is an essential tool for librarians: feel confident you are signposting safe, reliable, user-friendly online resources to students and teaching staff alike. We provide multi-user concurrent access, so no waiting around for another student to finish with a resource. Issues Online also provides FREE downloadable posters for your shelf/wall/table displays.

Teachers

Issues Online is an ideal resource for lesson planning, inspiring lively debate in class, and setting lessons and homework tasks.

Our accessible, engaging content helps deepen students' knowledge, promotes critical thinking, and develops independent learning skills.

Issues Online saves precious preparation time. We wade through the wealth of material on the internet to filter the best quality, most relevant and up-to-date information you need to start exploring a topic.

Our carefully selected, balanced content presents an overview and insight into each topic from a variety of sources and viewpoints.

Students

Issues Online is designed to support your studies in a broad range of topics, particularly social issues relevant to young people today.

There are thousands of articles, statistics and infographs instantly available to help you with homework, research, and assignments.

With 24/7 access using the powerful Algolia search system, you can find relevant information quickly, easily and safely anytime from your laptop, tablet or smartphone, in class or at home.

Visit issuesonline.co.uk to find out more!

Privacy

What is privacy?

Simply put, privacy is the ability to control access to your personal information and the power to keep your activities to yourself if you choose. It involves how our data is collected, stored, and used, how we communicate with others, and our ability to traverse digital spaces without unwarranted intrusion. It's not just about keeping secrets; it's about managing your own personal space, both online and off.

The right to privacy

The concept of privacy is so critical that it's protected by law in many countries. One key piece of legislation is found in the European Convention on Human Rights – specifically, Article 8: Right to privacy. It reads:

- Everyone has the right to respect for his private and family life, his home and his correspondence.

- There shall be no interference by a public authority with the exercise of this right except such as is in accordance with the law and is necessary in a democratic society in the interests of national security, public safety or the economic wellbeing of the country, for the prevention of disorder or crime, for the protection of health or morals, or for the protection of the rights and freedoms of others.

In this, the law outlines a fundamental respect for privacy while acknowledging that there may be times when your privacy could be overridden, like for safety or health reasons. However, any intrusion should be lawful and absolutely necessary, not random and unchecked.

Why is privacy important?

Personal freedom

Your individuality and freedom of expression flourish when you have privacy. It allows you to be you without the fear of being judged or monitored. Imagine constantly being watched or listened to – even the most confident person might start to second-guess themselves or feel uneasy about expressing their true thoughts.

Safety

With your personal information easily accessible online, your safety can be compromised. Information such as your home address, phone number, and even your current location can leave you vulnerable to stalking, identity theft, or worse.

Control over personal information

Privacy gives you the power to choose who knows what about you and when. It's about retaining control of your digital footprint, knowing that no one else is tracking your purchases, conversations, or browsing habits without your consent.

How is privacy threatened?

Unfortunately, in the digital world, there are countless ways your privacy can be compromised. Cyber threats like hacking, phishing, and malware are real dangers. Social media platforms can share your information with advertisers, and governments can surveil citizen communications for various reasons.

Being aware is the first step. But more importantly, being proactive about your online privacy is a must. Here's how you can protect yourself.

Protecting your privacy

Be aware of privacy settings

Most social media platforms and online services offer privacy settings that allow you to control who sees your information. Take the time to review and adjust these settings to safeguard your data.

Use strong passwords

Seems basic, right? However, many people still use passwords that are easy to guess. Use complex passwords and never use the same password for multiple accounts.

Think before you share

Once something is shared online, it's rather tough to take it back. Before posting that selfie or tweeting your thoughts, consider the potential long-term impact.

Stay informed

Laws and policies regarding privacy are always evolving. Stay informed about your rights and the ways companies or authorities might attempt to infringe upon them.

Use secure communications

Encryption isn't just for computer wizards. Apps that use end-to-end encryption make sure that only the person you're talking to can read what you send.

Minimise digital footprints

Be mindful of the trail you leave behind when you browse the web. Consider using privacy-focused browsers or search engines that don't track your activity.

A private and family life

Nobody should be able to secretly watch what we're doing without good reason – and we have the right to enjoy a family life in the way we choose.

Article 8 of the Human Rights Act protects our privacy, our family life, our home and our communications.

It's been used by families who've been unlawfully spied on by councils, won crucial rights for LGBT+ and trans people, and defended our fundamental freedoms in the face of increasingly authoritarian mass surveillance.

It means the State must not interfere with your right to privacy – though this can be limited in certain circumstances.

Your private life

The right to a private life protects your dignity and autonomy (your right to be independent and make your own decisions about your life).

That includes:

- respect for your sexuality

- the right to personal autonomy and physical and psychological integrity (this right means you must not t be physically or psychologically interfered with)

- respect for your private and confidential information, including the storing and sharing of data about you

- the right not to be subject to unlawful state surveillance

- the right to control the spreading of information about your private life, including photographs taken covertly.

Your family life

There's no set model of a family or family life. It includes any stable relationship – like those between romantic partners, parents and children, siblings or grandparents and grandchildren.

People often depend on this right when the State tries to separate family members – for example, by taking children into care or deporting somebody.

Respect for your home

You have a right not to have your home life interfered with, including by unlawful surveillance, unlawful entry and evictions which don't follow a proper process.

Respect for your correspondence

You have the right to uninterrupted and uncensored communication with others – a right that's particularly relevant when challenging phone tapping and the reading of your private communications.

Limitations

Article 8 can be limited in certain circumstances – but any limitation must balance the interests of an individual and of the community as a whole.

In particular, any limitation must be:

- covered by law

- necessary and proportionate

- for one or more of the following purposes:

  - public safety or the country's economic wellbeing

  - prevention disorder or crime

  - protecting health or morals

  - protecting other people's rights and freedoms.

  - national security.

Balancing rights

The right to privacy must often be balanced against the right to free expression.

Public figures don't necessarily enjoy the same privacy as other people do – sometimes public interest might justify publishing information about them that would otherwise interfere with the right to privacy.

Design

Design a poster highlighting Article 8.

Debate

As a class, debate privacy of public figures. Half of the class will be for the right to privacy for public figures and the other half against, for public interest.

Article 8 in action

10 NGOs V The United Kingdom

This case was brought by Liberty, Amnesty International, Privacy International and 11 other human rights and journalism groups – as well as two individuals – based in Europe, Africa, Asia and the Americas.

It was a five-year legal challenge to the UK's eye-wateringly broad and intrusive secret spying powers, first revealed by Edward Snowden.

In 2018, the European Court of Human Rights ruled that the UK's bulk interception regime had violated our rights to privacy under Article 8 – and to free expression, protected by Article 10.

The court found that intercepting communications data – the records of who, what, when, where and how we communicate – was as serious a breach of privacy as intercepting the content.

Judges also ruled that the UK's regime for authorising bulk interception was incapable of keeping the 'interference' with our rights to what is 'necessary in a democratic society'.

Jenny Paton's story

In 2008, Poole Council received an anonymous tip-off that Jenny Paton's family were lying about living in a certain school catchment area.

In fact, they'd lived there for more than 10 years – but that didn't stop their council subjecting them to James Bond-style undercover surveillance.

For three weeks officials sat outside Jenny's home, making notes and taking photographs. They even followed Jenny and her partner Tim while they drove their children to school.

The family had no idea – until the surveillance was exposed at a meeting with the council.

The Investigatory Powers Tribunal – the court that considers cases about state spying – found Poole Council had breached Article 8.

What is a digital footprint?

A footprint can leave a lasting impression, much like the information we post online. Read our top tips on making sure your online reputation is just as good as your offline one.

The photos we share, the comments we write, the videos we 'like' all say something about us to other people. Even if we delete them, they may still be out there – saved and shared by others, or even kept by the site or app itself.

What does the content you post online say about you?

As adults, this may have less of an effect on our futures, the people we meet online and the relationships we build, but for your child, the consequences could be far reaching.

Having been brought up in a digital world, your child's 'digital footprint' is likely to be much larger than yours. Most of us did things as teenagers that we wouldn't want people to have a photo or record of today. Most young people's lives are documented daily, by them, their friends and even their family, sometimes even before birth (ever seen a proud friend or relative share their ultrasound scan image on social media?).

How much room does this leave for children to make developmental mistakes, without having lasting proof and possible longstanding embarrassment?

Things to consider

- Embarrassment is one thing which young people may face but it's also possible that the things they post, or are posted about them, could have a negative effect on their reputation, education or future employment.

- Impact on school. Things that happen online, but involve fellow students, can be brought to the attention of their school, and children may be sanctioned as a result of their actions, even if they were not directly involved

in wrongdoing. They may have been a bystander who allowed bullying to take place, or perhaps liked or shared something they thought was funny, but which then caused harm or upset to others.

- Grooming and exploitation. In extreme cases, if your child has posted or shared sexual content, there is a possibility that they have shared this with strangers online without realising it. This could lead to them being pressured into continuing contact, or even being threatened into taking more images or meeting face to face.

- A digital footprint can also be a good thing. Your child can have a positive reputation online and there will be things that they do, such as volunteering or achievements, which they may want people (or future employers) to know about. The key is to have control over who and what people can find about them.

Five things to think about before you post

1. What do I look like?

If you didn't know you, what would you think about this post? What impression would you have of the person who posted it? Things that we might share with friends as a joke can look very different to someone else, and that might be someone you're trying to impress – a girl, a boy, even an employer or a college or university.

2. Is this permanent?

When you share something online, you can lose control of it. Even if you delete a photo or post you can't guarantee that it hasn't been copied or downloaded by someone else. Think about how many people you're sharing with and whether they'll be responsible with what you share. Don't forget it's easy for other people to copy what you share online, change it and share it without you knowing.

3. Am I giving away too much?

The more you share, the more people can learn about you. Could they use your posts to bully you or to trick you into sharing something you may not want the world to see?

4. Would I want this shared about me?

It's important to think about the impact what you post online might have on others. Do you have your friend's permission to share that funny picture of them? Could that jokey comment you posted hurt someone's feelings?

5. Does it pass the billboard test?

Before you post something online, think: would you be happy to see it on a billboard where the rest of your school, your parents, your grandparents and neighbours could see it? If not, do you really want to share it?

Five things to think about after you post

If your child still wants to share something online, what can they do to make sure they still have control over who sees it?

1. Mind your privacy

Most websites, apps and social networks you can share information on have 'privacy settings'. These help you control what you share, and who you share it with. So it's your choice

whether your friends, friends of friends, or everyone, can see a photo or comment.

2. Choose your friends wisely

It's always best to share only with friends you know in the real world. Remember too that what your friends share about you and their privacy settings online will also affect you and your digital footprint.

3. Remove and report

Think you shouldn't have made that comment? Make sure you know how to remove anything you regret posting from any sites you use. If someone's posted something about you that you're worried about and refuses to take it down, make sure you know how to report it.

4. Know what you look like online

'Google yourself now and again, and review your profiles on any social networks you use'

It can be hard to keep up with the things we've done online so it's a good idea to Google yourself now and again, and review your profiles on any social networks you use. That way you'll know what other people can find out about you, as well as things others might have posted about you.

5. Shut down or delete

If you stop using a social network, remember to shut down your profile or delete your account.

Design

Design a poster with tips on how to check your digital footprint.

Search...

Try searching for yourself on Google (or any other search engine) and see what results appear. Are they all about you, or do you share your name with someone else?

Why is your digital footprint important?

Each time you post a photo on social media, send an email to a colleague or use a search engine, you leave behind a traceable and permanent trail of data known as your 'digital footprint'.

Made up of all of your online activity, your footprint can be tracked, analysed, and used to construct a unique profile of you – including your location, social groups, behaviour and interests.

In fact, your footprint reveals so much about you that it's used by businesses to target you with personalised offers and advertisements, social media sites to segment you into groups, and by graduate employers looking to find information about you online before you meet.

But why is your digital footprint important?

Whether you upload an image to your social media profile or simply search for something on Google, anything that you do online has the potential to live forever.

Scary stuff, right? Well unfortunately if you use the internet, it's impossible to have no digital footprint at all.

If this is all sounding a little *Black Mirror*-esque to you, don't panic – because although you can't completely erase your digital footprint, you can reduce it and increase your privacy in a matter of moments, by following a few simple steps.

How to reduce your digital footprint

1. Google yourself

First of all, try entering your full name on a few different search engines and social media sites, and make a note of any results that aren't particularly favourable.

If you wouldn't be happy for a potential employer or a relative to see one of the results, contact the site administrator and ask for it to be taken down.

It's also possible to set up a Google Alert for your own name, so that you'll receive an alert message every time your name appears on the web.

2. Check your privacy settings

While social media sites like Facebook and Twitter can be great tools for networking, it's important to be aware that anything that is shared on your profile can be redistributed without your consent and also viewed by anyone (including a potential employer!).

To make sure that only people you know and trust are granted access to your page, change your privacy settings – and make sure that your social media profiles are a great representation of your own personal brand.

3. Create strong passwords

Every time you create a password, make sure that it uses a combination of letters (both upper and lower case), numbers and symbols, and don't just use the same password for every website.

Your passwords shouldn't be related to your name, birthday, or the names of close family or friends. And remember – never reveal your password to anyone!

4. Log out or deactivate

After you've finished using a website, make sure to log out – especially if you're using a shared computer.

And on that note, if you've decided that you don't want to use a website or an app anymore, always delete or deactivate your account rather than just close the site or delete the app, or you'll still be visible to other users.

It is also a good idea to deactivate old email addresses that you no longer use!

5. Read the T&Cs

This one's a long shot, we know. But if you're really serious about reducing your digital footprint, you should always read the Terms & Conditions to make sure that you're clued up on how that particular company will protect and share your information.

6. Opt-out

Don't tick the box to opt into third-party communications!

In fact, try to tick as few boxes as possible if you want to reduce your digital footprint.

If you have opted into something and changed your mind, simply unsubscribe or opt out! The EU General Data Protection Regulation (GDPR) now regulates data privacy online and allows you the right to be forgotten from communications or to have your data removed.

7. Use false data

If you don't want to give away personal data on a website, then don't!

Particularly if you are unsure about a website you are signing up to… Simply fake it and create false information such as a slightly different phone number, email address or date of birth.

There are some internet extensions or plugins out there that create 'digital noise' for you, leaving misleading and meaningless footprints on the web, weakening your 'real' data and making it harder for an algorithm to understand your footprint and ultimately reducing the opportunity for brands to manipulate you to make purchasing or other decisions online.

8. Be cautious before you click

If it looks like spam, it probably is spam! Think twice before you click on a link, even if it has been sent by a friend (they may have been hacked).

Clickbait is common in today's digital society.

Don't be fooled by the surveys you see pop up on Facebook, even if it just looks like a bit of fun. Remember that someone is collecting data about you from the way you answer.

9. Clear your cookies

Cookies are small bits of data created by websites – they're what allows a site to keep track of your online behaviour and customise your experience on the site based on how you use it.

If you want to make sure that you're browsing without leaving a trail of data, delete your cookies.

This will clear your user data and prevent sites from re-advertising products to you, and tracking your behaviour between sites.

Unfortunately, deleting your cookies each time you browse the internet will mean that you'll also have to re-enter your username and password every time you visit a website.

If that's sounding like it's going to be a headache, you can always take advantage of using a private browsing mode.

10. Think twice about what you post

What you post online can't easily be erased. Every status, like, retweet and Snapchat we send becomes part of our online record – so it's vital to ensure that everything you're sending conveys a positive message.

Before you post something online, think twice about whether it's something you would be happy to share with future employers, family members or clients.

The same applies to posting compromising photos of your friends – if you know that you'd be embarrassed by

something you're about to upload, then don't do it to someone else!

11. And finally – make sure that your footprint is positive

All this talk of data tracking and information sharing is sounding a bit dark, isn't it?

Well, panic not – because there is such a thing as a positive digital footprint, and if your name is going to be out there, why not use your digital footprint to create a favourable personal profile?

Think blog posts, fundraising pages, or even sharing articles on a subject you're interested in – these are exactly the kinds of things that graduate employers would be impressed by when they search your name online.

Your digital footprint can reveal a lot about your behaviour, interests and personality – and if you're on the hunt for a graduate job it's especially important to consider what it's saying about you.

So once you've followed our steps to cleaning up your digital footprint, remember that what you put out there is permanent – and make sure that you always leave a positive impression online.

2 January 2022

The above information is reprinted with kind permission from Give a Grad a Go.
© 2024 Give a Grad a Go

www.giveagradago.com

The impact your digital footprint could have on your career

A digital footprint refers to the trail of data each person leaves behind when using the internet. It can include the websites you visit to the emails you send or your passwords and social media posts. Every website you visit, pop-up ad you click on and social media post you make contribute to your digital footprint so it's impossible to use the internet without leaving a trail – it all contributes to your digital footprint, even if you apply for a job online and enter your national insurance number, you're adding to the print.

You can have both an active digital footprint and a passive digital footprint, your active digital footprint includes personal data you voluntarily share online. Things like – accepting a cookie on a new website, signing up for a newsletter or posting on social media. On the other hand, passive digital footprints include personal data that companies collect without your knowledge through things like third-party cookies and tracking scripts.

Digital footprints have such significance not just due to standing between you and your dream career, they last – once data becomes public such as an Instagram post, you have little to no control over its use by others. Secondly, a person's digital reputation which is now just as crucial as their offline reputation, can be determined by their digital footprint as content posted can easily be misinterpreted or manipulated, potentially causing unintended offence. Cybercriminals can even exploit people's digital footprints for phishing or identity theft purposes. So considering these factors, it becomes crucial to be mindful of the digital footprint we create. Many individuals actively manage their digital footprints by exercising caution in their online activities to control the data collected in the first place.

Employers, agencies, and recruiters carry out something called 'social media screening' which is looking through a potential candidate's social media profiles to help them find out whether they're suitable for the role. But if there's inappropriate content that could suggest otherwise online, that could potentially be jeopardising future career prospects. According to CareerBuilder, 2018 70% of employers conduct social media screening, meaning it's more important than ever to review your social media profiles before applying for your dream job.

Trying to delete your entire digital footprint completely is a complex task, but it's not impossible. To start you off, here are a few steps you can take to minimise its impact and manage your online presence. By going over all your online accounts and profiles – remove all unnecessary and outdated information so therefore it accurately reflects your current professional identity whilst reducing the risk of sharing any misleading information that might put off any recruiters of hiring managers. (It's also equally important to be cautious about any future content you plan on posting and whether it reflects your professional brand.)

Additionally, consider using online reputation management services or tools to monitor your digital presence and address any unwanted information that may appear online. By actively managing and curating your digital footprint, you take control of your online identity and present a positive and professional image to potential employers. Finally, don't forget to review and adjust your privacy settings on all platforms to limit the visibility of your personal information, further safeguarding your digital presence.

7 June 2023

Activity

Follow the advice in this article to check your digital footprint and to remove any damaging or out-of-date information about yourself.

Remember! It is best not to post anything that may harm your reputation, as it can sometimes be tricky to remove from some sites!

The above information is reprinted with kind permission from The Graduate Project.
© 2024 The Graduate Project

www.thegraduateproject.co.uk

Can I get fired for what I posted on social media?

Social media misuse can get you in serious trouble

Today, social media is a large part of people's lives. Be it Facebook, X, Instagram, LinkedIn or any other channel, 62% of people in the UK are active on some form of social media platform.

Although you may feel like your social and work lives are completely separate, you can actually face discipline or dismissal for social media misuse.

What is considered social media misuse?

The following would create grounds for an employment disciplinary:

- Posting negative comments about your job, clients or employer
- Sharing private company information
- Expressing off-colour personal opinions which could reflect badly on your employer
- Acting on behalf of the company without permission to do so

Private accounts

In the past year there has been uproar about certain social media sites' privacy policies, with lots of people learning that although their profiles seemed private, their personal data was actually being sold.

This was a wake-up call for many: the discovery that what was once thought to be personal was actually not at all shocked millions worldwide.

Similarly, even if your social media accounts are all private, what you post may be seen by a wider audience than you intended to reach.

A post which you think is only visible to your followers will not necessarily remain that way thanks to actions like screenshots.

Good news travels fast, but unfortunately so does bad news.

If you say something negative or derogatory about your employer – or even something which could damage their reputation – and someone sees and tells, you could wind up with a disciplinary action against you, or worse.

What is the law on social media misuse?

Although it might seem ridiculous that an employee could be fired over a Facebook comment or Tweet, the law in the UK upholds that misconduct on social media is taken as seriously as verbal misconduct in the workplace.

On the other hand, if you feel like you are a victim of bullying or prejudice from a colleague or employer via social media, employment laws are in place concerning social media misuse which could work to your advantage.

As social media becomes more prevalent in society, it is necessary for the law to adapt and accommodate employers who need to protect themselves and other employees against social media misuse.

Certain types of social media misuse may also involve breaches of the Equality Act 2010.

A dismissal for social media misuse would have to meet the test of fairness in the Employment Rights Act 1996.

Can posts from years ago be used against me?

Disciplinary or dismissal on the grounds of social media misuse does not have to refer to recent posts.

In fact, posts from years ago can come back to haunt employees if they resurface and are seen.

Unfortunately, employers may want to uphold a certain standard of reputation and will therefore not hesitate to distribute punishment for past posts.

Recent cases

As social media becomes more popular, companies are enforcing stricter social media policies.

Cases of companies dismissing employees, or employees resigning before the employer gets the chance to dismiss them for improper use of sites like Facebook and Twitter are on the rise.

Earlier this year Conservative party member Toby Young resigned just seven days after his appointment as a non-executive director on the board of the Office for Students due to controversy surrounding tweets he had made nearly a decade earlier.

Due to the nature of Young's tweets – which were labelled as racist, sexist and homophobic – his resignation was welcomed: if he had not resigned, it is doubtful he would have lasted long before being dismissed.

Another example of social media misuse leading to dismissal can be found in a case from last year in which API Microelectronics Limited fired one of their employees for joking on Facebook that she was going to 'sue them' after the company announced a possible relocation.

The employee – Mrs Plant – listed on her profile that she worked for API Microelectronics Limited, and thus her dismissal was ruled as fair since she could be associated with the company through her profile.

Unfair dismissal

However, not every dismissal claimed to be due to social media misuse is upheld.

An ongoing case concerning a civil servant in Blackburn has seen that he was unfairly dismissed last year for offensive activity on Twitter.

The employee in question accepted responsibility for his actions but claimed that he had been told during a security training presentation that if his Twitter account did not associate him to his employer, it didn't matter what he posted.

The employee's claim was not investigated and so even though he did breach company social media policy, Manchester employment tribunal has ruled that he was unfairly dismissed.

How can I be sure what I post is okay?

If you're employed by a company who value and respect the power social media can have then they should have a company social media policy, outlined for all employees and easily accessible.

The last thing you want is to be punished or dismissed, so it is definitely worth checking over the policy in place to make sure you are on the same wavelength as the company or person who employs you.

To be on the safe side, if you have the slightest doubt that what you're about to post is acceptable then just leave it!

We all know that work can be really frustrating at times, but it is wise to find another outlet to express your discontent into.

It goes without saying that any racist, sexist, homophobic, transphobic, disablist, illegal or otherwise derogatory online activity will land you in deep trouble.

The above information is reprinted with kind permission from Cartwright King.

© 2024 AWH Acquisition Corp Ltd T/A Cartwright King

www.cartwrightking.co.uk

What is online safety and why is it important?

In the digital age, our lives are increasingly conducted online. From social interactions and entertainment to shopping and banking, the internet has become a central hub for a myriad of activities. However, this convenience also brings with it a range of risks and vulnerabilities. Online safety, or cyber safety, refers to the practices and precautions taken to protect personal information and ensure a secure environment while navigating the digital world. Understanding what online safety entails and its significance is crucial in today's interconnected society.

The essence of online safety

Online safety encompasses a broad spectrum of measures aimed at safeguarding users' personal, financial, and professional information from theft, abuse, and mismanagement. It involves protecting one's identity, data, and devices against cyber threats such as viruses, malware, phishing scams, cyberbullying, and identity theft. To achieve this, online safety practices include the use of strong, unique passwords, the installation of antivirus software, regular software updates, cautious sharing of personal information, and awareness of the latest online scams.

At its core, online safety is about creating a secure online presence that minimises vulnerabilities and maximises user confidence in engaging with digital platforms. This not only protects the individual but also contributes to the overall security of the digital ecosystem by preventing the spread of malicious activities and software.

Why online safety is paramount

The importance of online safety cannot be overstated. In an era where data is a valuable commodity, the repercussions of data breaches and identity theft can be devastating. Personal, financial, and professional damages can occur, leading to significant emotional and monetary losses. Furthermore, the ubiquity of social media and digital communication platforms has given rise to concerns over privacy, cyberbullying, and misinformation, making online safety a critical component of digital literacy.

Moreover, businesses and economies at large are also at risk. Cyberattacks can disrupt operations, erode customer trust, and entail hefty recovery costs. In essence, ensuring online safety is vital for maintaining the integrity of personal and corporate data, fostering trust in digital transactions, and supporting the overall health of the digital economy.

Building a culture of online safety

Promoting online safety requires a collective effort. Individuals need to stay informed about potential online risks and adopt best practices for digital hygiene. Parents and educators play a crucial role in teaching children and young adults about the importance of being safe and responsible online. Businesses and organisations, for their part, must invest in robust cybersecurity measures and promote a culture of awareness and vigilance among their employees.

Governmental and non-governmental organisations can also contribute by advocating for safer digital environments, supporting cybersecurity initiatives, and enacting laws and regulations that protect online users while respecting privacy and freedom of expression.

Conclusion

The internet has transformed how we work, learn, play, and interact. Yet, with these benefits come challenges that necessitate a commitment to online safety. By understanding and implementing cyber safety measures, we can protect ourselves and contribute to a safer, more secure digital world for everyone. As technology continues to evolve, so will the landscape of online threats, making ongoing education and adaptation to new safety practices imperative. Ultimately, online safety is not just a personal responsibility but a collective one that is essential for preserving the freedoms and opportunities that the digital age offers.

15 cybercrime statistics you ought to know

By Camille Dubuis-Welch

Unless you live off-grid and offline, you'll be familiar with cybercrime. It's likely you've even been the victim of a cyber attack already – though you might not be aware of it.

With just shy of six billion electronic records being stolen globally, according to the latest Mimecast Email and Collaboration Security report, the world of cybercrime is vast and, for those attempting to understand and resolve it, the landscape is ever-changing. From receiving a shady text from the Post Office to having your email compromised following your Ferrari upgrade, letting your guard down online simply isn't an option.

While a good VPN combined with up-to-date anti-virus software will cover your IP address and give you more general peace of mind while browsing, when it comes to protecting yourself from cybercrime, there's always more that can be done. Cybercrime is by no means new and some of the most prominent cases – such as WannaCry, Petya, NotPetya which disrupted at least 81 English health trusts and cancelled nearly 19,494 medical appointments – date back to 2017 with continued impact.

It's a battle for individuals and smaller companies just as much as it is for big organisations; as the digital space is expanding and as AI is impacting our everyday lives, hackers are getting more inventive every day. And, if you're not convinced that cybercrime is going to be an issue in your life, the statistics below will change your mind.

It seems that the UK is ripe for cybercrime. Currently second on the Global Cyber Security Index behind the US, here are some stats that make it clear why better prevention and general management of cyber threats is more essential than ever.

1. Half of businesses (50%) experienced some form of cyber security breach in 2023

A survey by the Department for Science, Innovation & Technology showed that one in two businesses reported a cyber breach or attack in the last 12 months, while almost a third of charities (32%) reported the same.

These figures are much higher for medium businesses, where 70% experienced a cyber breach, large businesses (74%), and charities with yearly incomes of £500,000 or higher (66%).

2. Phishing attacks were the most disruptive in 2023

According to the UK Official Statistics Cyber Security Breaches report 2023, 61% of businesses and 56% of charities reported that staff receiving fraudulent emails or using fraudulent websites was the most disruptive cyber security breach.

This was followed by people impersonating their organisation or staff in emails or online.

3. Four cyber security reports last year were among the most severe incidents the National Cyber Security Centre (NCSC) has ever had to manage

According to NSCS's annual review, there were 2,005 cyber security incidents in 2023 – an increase of 64% from the previous year. Of these, 62 were nationally significant, and four were among the most severe incidents the NCSC has had to manage (compared with one last year) due to the sustained disruption they caused and the victims' links to critical infrastructure via supply chains.

4. 32% of UK businesses are attacked at least once a week

According to the UK Official Statistics Cyber Security Breaches report 2023, 32% of businesses and 20% of charities note

Phishing attacks were the most distruptive in 2023

50%
of businesses experienced some form of cyber security breach in 2023

£1,630
Average short-term costs of cyber breaches or attacks for UK businesses

Source: independent.co.uk

4 cyber security reports last year were among the most severe incidents the National Cyber Security Centre (NCSC) has ever had to manage

2023: 2,005 cyber security reported incidents

32%
of businesses in the UK are attacked at least once a week

cyber attacks as frequently as once a week. 7% of businesses even reported they experienced cyber attacks as commonly as several times a day.

5. Cyber breaches or attacks cost UK businesses on average £1,630 in short-term costs

In organisations that identified breaches with an outcome, the average cost of cybercrime for UK businesses for short-term expenses (payments to external IT consultants, any payments to the attackers, money stolen) reported by the UK government is £1,630. This figure stands at £4,250 for medium and large businesses. The figure for micro/small UK businesses was £1,450, and £1,130 for charities.

10 global cybercrime statistics for 2024

Money is a huge motivation for cyber attacks around the world. According to Steve Morgan, editor-in-chief at Cybersecurity Ventures, if cybercrime was measured as a country, it would be the world's third largest economy, behind the US and China. Now to see what else has been happening beyond the UK, and no doubt shaping the cybersecurity landscape.

1. Cybercrime costs could reach US$10.5 trillion (£8.4 trillion GBP) annually by 2025

According to Cybersecurity Ventures, damage costs are set to increase by 15% per year until 2025 where estimates predict that global expenditure on cybercrime could reach US$10.5 trillion (£8.4 trillion).

Top 10 countries by cybercrime density

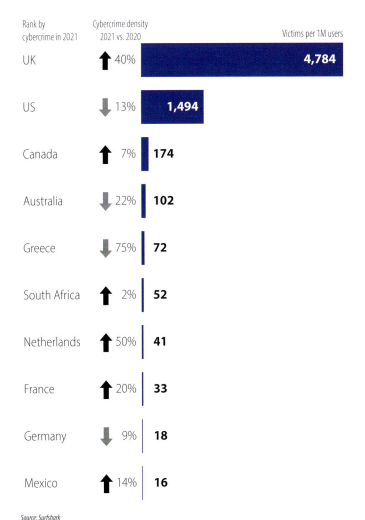

Rank by cybercrime in 2021	Cybercrime density 2021 vs. 2020	Victims per 1M users
UK	↑ 40%	4,784
US	↓ 13%	1,494
Canada	↑ 7%	174
Australia	↓ 22%	102
Greece	↓ 75%	72
South Africa	↑ 2%	52
Netherlands	↑ 50%	41
France	↑ 20%	33
Germany	↓ 9%	18
Mexico	↑ 14%	16

Source: Surfshark

2. Cybercrime is expected to grow by 15% this year

According to the Mimecast Email and Collaboration Security report, cybercrime is expected to surge by 15% throughout 2024, going from a global total of US$8 trillion (£6.2 trillion) in 2023 to a projected US$10.5 trillion (£8.2 trillion) by the end of 2025. This number sat at US$3 trillion (£2.3 trillion) in 2015.

3. There was a 27% increase in hacktivism, data theft and initial access broker (IAB) activity against police in Q3 2023

Hacktivism, where hackers pursue political agendas through cyber attacks, continued to gain momentum during Q3 in 2023, with public safety organisations emerging as prime targets, as revealed by the Public Safety Threat Alliance (PSTA). During that time, hacktivist threats accounted for 83% of all cyber activities targeting the public safety sector.

Law enforcement agencies experienced a 28% surge in cybercrime incidents, primarily fuelled by hacktivism and financial motivations.

4. Companies took an average of 277 days to identify and contain a security breach in 2023

According to IBM's 2023 report, it takes an average of 277 days for those on the frontline of security to identify and respond to a security breach. This is the same amount of time as in 2022 but 10 days fewer than in 2021.

The longer it takes to identify and contain a cyber attack, the more expensive it is. The 2023 report also shows an average cost saving of US$1.02 million (£801,862) – 23% – for breaches that took less than 200 days to contain.

5. Ransomware damages cost 57 times more in 2021 than in 2015: US$20 billion (£16 billion)

According to Cybersecurity Ventures' 2023 report, ransomware could cost victims (consumers and organisations) around US$265 billion (£212 billion) annually by 2031, with new attacks as frequent as every two seconds. In 2021, it was estimated damages were US$20 billion (£16 billion). The UK's NCSC chief executive officer, Lindy Cameron, believes ransomware could now be the most immediate cybersecurity threat to UK businesses.

6. Hackers attack your computer every 39 seconds

A Clark School study, conducted by Michel Cukier in a bid to profile 'brute force' hackers, showed that attacks are happening all the time on computers with an internet connection, averaging 2,244 attempts a day and amounting to one attack every 39 seconds. Although not all successful, most are trying to access usernames and passwords.

7. Data breaches cost businesses an average of US$4.45 million (£3.49 million) in 2023

There are a number of ways that data can be compromised, and many companies are falling victim to data breaches. According to IBM's study, data breaches have become increasingly costly, with the average breach setting organisations back a record-breaking US$4.45 million (£3.49 million) in 2023 – a 2.3% increase from the US$4.35 million average cost in 2022.

Looking back over a longer time frame, the financial toll of data breaches has increased by 15.3% since 2020, when the average cost stood at $3.86 million.

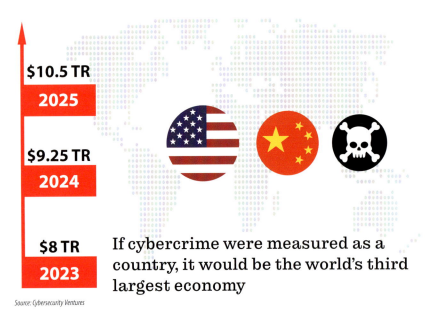

$10.5 TR
2025

$9.25 TR
2024

$8 TR
2023

If cybercrime were measured as a country, it would be the world's third largest economy

Source: Cybersecurity Ventures

8. Over 353 million US individuals were affected by compromised data in 2023

The effects of cybercrime and data breaches are expansive and global. According to Statista studies, there were 3,205 cases of data compromises on US individuals last year, and 353 million individuals were in some way affected by threat actors.

9. 61% of organisations were targeted with email phishing attacks in 2023

Email phishing is the most common type of attack, SoSafe's Cybercrime Trends Report 2024 tells us. Although, the report also reveals the cyber threat landscape is rapidly evolving, with 34% of attacks now leveraging social media platforms. This trend poses a significant risk, particularly for small businesses that heavily rely on social media to attract and engage customers. Cybercriminals are exploiting this vulnerability, hijacking business accounts and essentially crippling their operations.

10. The average cost of a breach in the healthcare industry is roughly US$10.93 million (£8.5 million), increasing from US$10.10 million (£8.1 million) in 2022

According to IBM's 2023 report, healthcare is regarded as one of the most highly regulated industries in the US and, for the 13th consecutive year, remains the costliest industry for data breaches. The cost of a data breach for the healthcare industry in 2023 was estimated at US$10.93 million (£8.5 million), 53.3% higher than it was in 2020.

The following top four industries by costs incurred are the financial, pharmaceutical, energy, and industrial sectors. Notably, IBM's threat intelligence data reveals that the manufacturing industry emerges as the most frequent target for cybercriminal activities.

Into the trillions

It's becoming clear that learning from failures and staying one step ahead of the cybercriminals is what will help victims come out on top, but with cybercrime set to cost the world $13.8 trillion dollars (£10.8 trillion) by 2028, there is still some work to be done.

Costs resulting from cybercrimes are not just fraud on a public or private company level; the impacts can be expansive. Pauses in productivity, lawsuits from data compromises and long-term effects of stolen business intelligence for organisations, not to mention reputational harm, all add up. For example, the MOVEit ransomware attacks that occurred in June 2023 impacted millions of individuals and thousands of organisations. Through the payment of ransomware demands, the cybercriminal group ClOP, is estimated to have amassed millions of dollars, according to the World Economic Forum's Global Cybersecurity Outlook January 2024 Insight Report.

The rise of ransomware

When it comes to the different types of cybercrime, there are many. Malware, phishing, ransomware and disrupted denial of service attacks (DDoS) are some of the most common.

The NCSC's annual report highlights ransomware as one of the biggest threats to domestic organisations, taking up a lot of its efforts. Between September 2022 and August 2023, the NCSC received 297 reports of ransomware activity. However, the threat landscape is seeing a rise in data extortion attacks, where cybercriminals steal sensitive information without encrypting it.

The NCSC believes these threats will only increase with AI becoming more widely available. The Rt Hon Oliver Dowden CBE MP says:

'The rapid rise of artificial intelligence (AI) is accelerating the pace of change, compounding the threats and lowering the barrier to entry. As a result, the cyber world is a more dangerous place than ever before, and cyber security is rising up our risk register.'

The latest targets

IBM's X-Force Threat Intelligence Index 2024 details that the manufacturing sector is the most at risk of cyber attacks, with the industry experiencing 25.7% of incidents within the top 10 industries throughout 2023. Finance and insurance (18.2%) was the second-most attacked industry and professional, business and consumer services (15.4%) were the third.

Safeguarding the future

It's clear that bigger companies, which have access to more funding and better resources, can absorb the cybercrime costs more easily. A 2023 ITRC Business Impact report found that 73% of US small businesses had experienced a cyber breach or data attack in 2023. From these, 13% of owners said these attacks cost the business more than US$500,000 (£393,225).

Outside of the costs of dealing with a cyber attack, ransom payments differed between business sizes. According to Sophos' The State of Ransomware 2024 report, smaller companies with annual revenues under US$10 million (£7.8 million) are less likely to pay ransoms, with only 25% of such firms reporting having made ransom payments. Whereas larger companies with revenues exceeding US$5 billion (£3.9 billion) have the highest ransom payment rate at 61%.

However, a key factor influencing this will most likely be the availability of funds, as many small businesses simply lack the financial resources to cover the ransom demands.

The NSCS's annual review 2023 highlights how important it is to improve the UK's cyber resilience to significant cyber risks to safeguard the country's infrastructure. The organisation is looking to continue building an understanding of the cyber threats to both businesses and individuals.

Furthermore, the National Cybersecurity Strategy report released by the US Biden-Harris Administration highlights a want to better support vulnerable individuals and small businesses in cyberspace. The report, released 2 March 2023, notes how the US is preparing to invest US$65 billion into a safe and reliable internet and outlines plans to bolster online defences to create a secure digital environment.

Embracing the unexpected

As we continue in 2024, many say that we're going to see more unusual cases of cybercrime attacks. Therefore, companies need to set the pace when it comes to cybercrime and emphasise vigilance while actively building defence systems and not giving threat actors easy or obvious targets.

According to Proofpoint's 2024 report, only 59% of employees were either unsure or claimed they weren't responsible for security in their companies.

This is set to shift. An awareness of how cyberminds are working in the modern age will be key to understanding the future of cyberattacks and defence, according to cyber expert Bruce Schneier, Harvard University.

However, knowing which will take precedence in the short and long term remains uncertain. Some experts say businesses might even want to fall back onto 'classic' cybersecurity skills. Founder and CEO of Hack The Box, Haris Pylarinos, predicts: 'I expect to see a growing demand for retro cybersecurity skills, as businesses revert to old, cheaper ways of working while cybercriminals use modern skills to hack into legacy technology,' anticipating the best ways that business can outdo hackers this year.

It will be crucial for companies to get the right type of cyber insurance and make phishing and other types of cyber attack tests for employees as ritualistic as fire drills. Future strategy is also about building a supportive and security-first environment; using AI for threat intelligence or for enhanced risk assessments; implementing extended detection and response (xdr); considering a healthy zero trust architecture (which saved some companies an average of US$1 million in average breach costs); and exploring more paths that can contribute to lower data breach costs and shorter identification times.

If you own a small UK business, there are still lots of affordable ways to protect your company, the NCSC has a sound online resource you can utilise. That being said, there is a four million shortage of cyber-professionals, so there is definitely room for those who are up for the challenge of outsmarting cybercriminals beyond 2024.

Quick steps to stay protected online

There are a few simple steps you can take to ensure you've got the basics covered when it comes to protecting yourself or your place of work from cybercrime. As well as staying aware of the latest data breaches and crimes in the UK and further afield, here are some more tips to consider:

1. Check your emails carefully

Keep your guard up against phishing links and leads on email, text or via any manner of communication for that matter. Note that unsolicited emails may be designed to look like your bank or a reputable industry/service like the NHS or Post Office in the UK. Check authenticity by analysing the domain name (the text after @ symbol) matches the website before clicking any links or opening attachments.

If you do still want to open an attachment from an email like this, which isn't recommended, scan it with anti-virus first. Bear in mind that even what might appear as a seemingly harmless PDF file can be an app in disguise and install nasty malware on your computer or phone. Also note that your bank will be able to let you know how to recognise a legitimate email or other type of communication from them so confirm directly before getting caught out.

2. Protect your data with a VPN

Especially when using public wifi or when connecting to a sensitive website such as your bank or pension provider. There are even some reputable free VPNs that can protect you without breaking the bank.

3. Use hard-to-crack passwords

Update passwords regularly and make them complex. Cybersecurity experts at McAfee suggest updating all passwords at least every three months to reduce the chances of hacking.

4. Keep apps and software updated

Keeping your apps and software up to date on your laptop, mobile phone, and other devices will minimise the risk of hackers finding faults in your system to easily access files or mess about with any online security settings.

5. Stay secure and vigilant on social media

Keeping settings private. If you typically use your pet(s)' name(s) as the answer to basic security questions online, keep it under wraps or reconsider. If you have kids, ensure they are aware of how to stay safe online too and make sure they feel confident in talking to you if they come across or are subjected to any form of harassment or cyberbullying.

Generally speaking, it's better to be safe than sorry. Some banks don't reimburse money lost if you have given your data away so it's important you can spot the signs and avoid cybercrime at all costs.

28 June 2024

Privacy settings

Why is privacy online important?

Every time we share something online we add a bit more information about ourselves to the online world. This includes posting a photo, writing a comment or liking someone's video.

The trail of information we create when we share things online is often called our 'digital footprint'. People we know, and people we don't know, can see our digital footprint and use it to learn more about us.

This means sometimes people can see things online or learn things about us we don't want them to see or know.

How can I protect my privacy online?

You can take control of your digital footprint by using privacy settings.

Privacy settings help you to choose who can see what you post and share.

Privacy settings are usually located under 'Settings' or 'My Account' on devices, apps and websites.

What restrictions can I apply?

Different devices, apps and websites let you control different things. Some restrictions you can apply are:

- You can make your account private
- You can turn off location tracking or limit when this happens
- You can control who can see things you post
- You can control who can comment on things you post
- You can control who can share things you post
- You can control who can tag you in posts
- You can control who can send you private messages
- You can control who can search for and find your account
- You can limit what information the platform stores about you

Sometimes apps offer a 'privacy check-up or review' to help you look at the most important privacy settings.

Tips for protecting your privacy online

1 **Know who you are sharing your information with.** Think about who you want to be able to see what you are posting.

2 **Know what you look like online.** Google yourself to see what other people can find about you.

3 **Remember that what your friends post affects you too.** Things they post about you adds to your digital footprint.

4 **Review your social media profiles regularly.** See if there is anything you want to delete or that you'd rather no one else could see.

5 **Delete old accounts.** These might have old pictures, videos or information you no longer want to share with the online world.

Max your online safety!

Find out how to block the trolls, swerve the scammers and deal with nudes with our online safety tips.

Trolls

Trolling is when someone deliberately makes a comment or shares a picture or post online with the sole purpose of upsetting, angering or teasing another person. Trolling is a form of cyber-bullying.

The best way to deal with trolls is to ignore and block them. They feed on attention, and, without it, they often get bored and move on. Here's a 4-step plan to beat the trolls:

1. Never feed a troll. Try to resist the temptation to respond to their comments or to engage with them at all.

2. Always take a screenshot just in case you do need to take the issue further. You might need to report the troll at some point so it's always handy to have evidence of their original post.

3. Many celebrities and influencers experience trolls every single day. Their social media feeds are full of hurtful, negative comments about their appearance and personal lives. If you see a trolling comment, don't engage. Simply ignore, report and block.

4. If you receive a particularly nasty comment from a troll which makes you feel threatened or frightened for your own safety, you should tell an adult immediately. You can then report it to the social media platform and the police, if necessary.

Sexting & nudes

Sexting is when you send explicit messages or texts or share images of your body. It's important to know the law around sending nudes or sexualised messages. If you are under 18, it is illegal for anyone to share sexualised images of you. It is also illegal for someone to send sexualised images to you. If you are over 18, it is against the law for someone to share pictures of you without your consent. There are laws and support in place to help you.

'I'm being asked to send nudes…'

It's important to know that it's never OK for someone to pressure you into sending sexual images or messages. If you have sent something and you're worried about what might happen, you can get more advice here.

'Someone is threatening to share the nude photos they have of me…'

If someone is threatening to share your nudes, this is against the law. If you are under 18 and someone is threatening to share images of you, you must tell an adult straight away. If you are over 18 and someone has posted an image or video of you without your permission, you can get help from the Revenge Porn Helpline: https://revengepornhelpline.org.uk/

'Someone has sent me an unwanted nude pic…'

If you've been sent a nude image or something that makes you feel uncomfortable, end the conversation and tell an adult you trust. It can be shocking and upsetting to open a message to find a sexually explicit image that you did not want to see. You need the support and help of a parent or adult to help you deal with it.

Catfishes

Catfishing is when someone uses someone else's photos or information to pretend to be someone they're not. It can be difficult to spot a catfish but here are some tips to help prevent you from being catfished:

* Be careful who you befriend on social media. Make a simple rule of not accepting friend requests from people you've never met in real life. A profile picture may seem perfectly innocent and show a teenager who looks a lot like you, but you never know who could be behind the account.

* Look at their account to see if it appears to be legitimate. Red flags include a newly created account, minimal interaction on their newsfeed and very few photos of themselves.

* Never give money to someone who asks for it online.

* Set your social accounts to 'private'.

Scammers

Scam emails and sites are often easy to spot, but the more sophisticated scams can be tricky to identify. If something seems too good to be true, then that's because it usually is. To stay safe, you can:

* Check emails, texts and websites properly before clicking any links and look for misspelled words or bad punctuation as these are often indicators that the communication is not genuine.

* Be wary of phishing emails and attempts – this is when someone tries to steal your personal information to gain access to your accounts. Always check with an adult if you're unsure about anything you see, read or receive online. Trust your gut and be cautious if you suspect something isn't quite right.

* Be cautious of any 'urgent' emails or messages telling you things like, 'you have 24 hours to respond' or 'failure to respond will mean you incur a fine'. This type of threatening email is most usually a criminal scam.

* Use passwords to keep your personal information safe. Try to use different passwords for different accounts and make them hard to guess to increase your security.

* Not sure if an email is a scam? If you have received an email which you're not quite sure about, forward it to report@phishing.gov.uk to be checked over.

8 February 2022

How to create the perfect password

Why your password matters

Imagine if someone had the key to your diary, your private messages, or even your bank account. Scary, right? That's essentially what happens when someone gets a hold of one of your passwords. They can steal your information, impersonate you, or even lock you out of your own accounts. Think of your password as a digital lock that keeps the bad guys out of your personal space.

The recipe for a perfect password

A good password is like a secret code that only you can understand. It should be hard for others to guess but easy for you to remember. Here's how to cook up a strong password:

1. The longer, the better

Start with length. A strong password should be at least 12 characters long. Longer passwords are harder for hackers to crack. Think of them as the boss level in a video game that takes extra effort to conquer.

2. Mix it up

Your password should be a cocktail of letters (both uppercase and lowercase), numbers, and symbols. Just like mixing different ingredients can create an amazing smoothie, mixing different characters can make your password strong and hard to guess.

3. Avoid the obvious

Using your name, birthday, or 'password' as your password is like leaving your front door unlocked. It's inviting trouble. Avoid any personal information that someone could easily find or guess.

4. Be unpredictable

Don't use the same password everywhere. If a hacker gets a hold of one password, you don't want them to have the key to all your accounts. Mix it up and keep them guessing.

Creating a strong password: the fun part

Here's where we turn the mundane task of creating a password into a game. Instead of random, hard-to-remember strings of characters, think of a phrase or a sentence that means something to you. For example, the sentence 'My two dogs barked too loud for the neighbours!' can turn into a password like 'M2dB2L4tN!'. It's long, uses a mix of characters, and is unique to you.

Gameify your password

Song lyrics: Pick a line from your favourite song. For instance, 'Hit me baby one more time!' could be 'HmB1mt!'

Movie quotes: Use a memorable line from a movie, like 'May the force be with you' could become 'MtFbwU4!'

Book titles: Combine book titles and the year you read them. 'Harry Potter and the Philosopher's Stone 2001' could be 'HP&tPs2oo1!'

Tools to the rescue

If you're still stuck, or if keeping track of all your awesome passwords is turning into a nightmare, consider using a password manager. These handy tools not only generate strong passwords for you but also store them securely. All you need to remember is one master password to access them all.

The don'ts of password creation

- Don't write your passwords down on a piece of paper that could easily be lost or seen by someone you don't trust.

- Don't share your passwords with friends or significant others. Your privacy is important.

- Don't use the same password across multiple sites. Once one account is compromised, all of them could be at risk.

Final thoughts

In the grand scheme of things, creating a unique and strong password is one of the simplest yet most effective ways to safeguard your digital life. As you embrace the online world, taking a few minutes to craft a solid password is like investing in a good lock for your door – it provides security and peace of mind.

Remember, the effort you put into creating your passwords is a reflection of how much you value your online presence and personal information. So, take these tips, get creative, and start building those digital fortresses one unique, strong password at a time. Happy securing!

QR Codes – what's the real risk?

How safe is it to scan that QR code in the pub? Or in that email?

By David C

QR codes have been around since the 90s, although in the UK they really came to prominence during Covid-19 lockdowns where they were used for everything from ordering food to indicating vaccination status.

They're widely used today for things like quickly directing users to websites, logging into devices that lack keyboards (such as online video services on smart devices), or ordering or paying for goods and services.

Understandably, people sometimes worry about whether to trust these QR codes. Many are used in public spaces (like pubs and restaurants), and so you might be wondering: are criminals placing malicious QR codes to steal money, information, or trick people in some way?

Reports of QR-enabled fraud in the UK can be found online (including one from BBC News where a woman was scammed at a railway station), but this type of scam is relatively small compared to other types of cyber fraud. The majority of QR code-related fraud tends to happen in open spaces (like stations and car parks), and often involves an element of social engineering. In the above example, criminals posing as bank staff rang the victim to continue the deception.

However, QR codes are increasingly being used in phishing emails (a technique sometimes called 'quishing'). From the criminal's perspective, using QR codes in this way makes sense, for a number of reasons.

1. Most people are now suspicious of dubious-looking links in emails, and are (correctly) cautious of clicking on shortened links. Criminals are therefore using QR codes to disguise the links to malicious websites that phishing emails contain.

2. Not all security tools designed to detect phishing emails will scan images, so a QR code directing the user to a malicious website might slip through.

3. Users are more likely to use their personal phone to scan the QR code. Personal devices may not have the same security protections as a computer that's provided by your employer.

To summarise:

- The QR codes used in pubs or restaurants are probably safe for you to scan.

- Scanning QR codes in open spaces (like stations and car parks) might be riskier. As with many cyber attacks, you should be suspicious if you're asked to provide what feels like too much information, whether that's on a website or in any follow-up communications (such as a phone call).

- If you receive an email with a QR code in it, and you're asked to scan it, you should exercise caution as the NCSC is seeing an increase in these types of 'quishing' attacks.

Finally, we recommend that you use the QR-scanner that comes with your phone, rather than using an app downloaded from an app store.

8 February 2024

SCAN ME!

The QR code scam leaving victims thousands out of pocket

One victim scammed out of £13,000 in a QR code sham at Teeside car park.

By Jabed Ahmed

A woman has been left thousands of pounds out of pocket as part of a new QR code scam that is sweeping the country.

The number of QR code scams in the UK has soared, with over 400 reported this year and 1,200 investigated by Action Fraud since 2020.

In a recent scam, fraudsters covered a genuine QR code with a fake one in Thornaby Station's car park, Teeside.

The QR code took one 71-year-old victim to a fake website, allowing scammers to find out her payment and card information.

The victim's bank blocked a string of fraudulent transactions, but the scammers called her impersonating the bank and persuaded her they were real to get more information.

With the extra details, they changed the victim's address on her bank records and created a new online account.

They then racked up £13,000 in debt under her name, including a £7,500 loan and multiple credit cards, the BBC reports.

TransPennine Express, which runs the station and more than 100 others, has decided to remove all QR codes from its car parks following similar scams across the country.

Speaking to BBC, the victim, who asked to remain anonymous, described the ordeal as a 'logistical nightmare' as she is still waiting for her credit card to be unfrozen.

She said: 'I can't believe I fell for it. I've had so many sleepless nights and spent hours and hours speaking to my bank and credit card company trying to sort it all.

'I was locked out of my accounts. Luckily I had another credit card to survive on, but without that and help from my son, I don't know how I would have coped.'

VirginMoney said that all of the transactions had since been refunded and the loan cancelled. It said they have taken steps to protect the woman's account in the future.

18 November 2023

Understanding phishing, vishing, and smishing

In today's digital era, it's not uncommon to hear about various scams and cyber threats that lurk in the shadows of our online world. As a teenager who likely spends a considerable amount of time browsing the web, gaming, or engaging on social media, it's crucial to stay informed about these deceptive practices. Let's dive into the details of phishing, vishing, and smishing – three common forms of digital deception you might encounter – and discuss how you can guard against them.

Phishing: don't take the bait

Phishing is a cybercrime where targets are contacted by email, telephone, or text message by someone posing as a legitimate institution to lure individuals into providing sensitive data. This data could include personally identifiable information, banking and credit card details, or passwords.

The term 'phishing' plays on the word 'fishing'; the scammers throw out their 'baits' (usually, a deceptive email) hoping that someone will 'bite'. The emails often look real, with official logos and language that make you think it's from a company or person you trust.

How to avoid phishing:

- Be sceptical: if an email asks for sensitive information, it's a red flag. Legitimate companies don't ask for this information via email.

- Check the sender's email address: look closely at the sender's email. It might mimic a reputable company but with slight alterations, like 'amaz0n.com' instead of 'amazon.com'.

- Don't click on suspicious links: if an email contains a link, hover over it to see where it actually leads before clicking. Better yet, go directly to the website in question by typing the address into your browser.

- Keep your computer secure: use antivirus software, keep your system up-to-date, and don't disable firewall protections.

- Educate yourself: learn about the latest phishing scams and teach your friends and family, so they know what to look out for.

Vishing: voice + phishing

Vishing, a portmanteau of 'voice' and 'phishing', is phishing's auditory counterpart. Here, scammers use phone calls to trick you into providing personal information. They might claim to be from a bank, a computer tech support team, or any other entity that might have a reason to contact you.

These criminals are cunning and may use threat tactics, like claiming your account is compromised or that you owe money, to pressure you into sharing information without thinking it through.

How to avoid vishing:

- Don't trust caller id: caller ids can be spoofed. Just because it looks like a local number or a legitimate company is calling doesn't mean it's not a scammer on the other end.

- Never give out personal information: never give out personal information over the phone unless you initiated the call to a number you are sure is correct.

- Hang up and call back: if you are unsure about the legitimacy of a call, hang up and call the company or organisation back using a verified phone number.

- Be wary of urgency: scammers often create a sense of urgency. Take a moment to think and do your research before responding.

Smishing: sms + phishing

Smishing is like phishing but carried out through sms (text messaging) or messaging apps. Here, scammers send out texts designed to trick you into clicking on a link, replying with personal information, or downloading a malicious app.

The messages might alert you to a 'problem' with your bank account or credit card, or they might offer a 'prize' or 'reward' that's too good to be true. Just like phishing emails, they use the same urgent language to spur you into action.

How to avoid smishing:

- Don't click on links in text messages: if you receive a text with a link, do not click on it. If you think it might be legitimate, independently search for the company's website and contact them directly.

- Don't reply to suspicious texts: if you reply, scammers will know your number is active, which might lead to more messages or calls.

- Install security software on your smartphone: security apps can often detect and block harmful texts and calls.

- Block unknown numbers: if you receive messages from an unknown number that seem suspicious, block the number.

- Beware of 'too good to be true' offers: if an offer seems too good to be true, it usually is. Be cautious when approached with these kinds of texts.

- Most phone providers are part of a scheme that allows customers to report suspicious text messages for free by forwarding it to 7726. If you forward a text to 7726, your provider can investigate the origin of the text and arrange to block or ban the sender, if it's found to be malicious.

The bottom line

Phishing, vishing, and smishing all aim to steal your information or money without you noticing. Being aware of these scams and knowing how to handle suspicious messages or calls is your best defence. Remember, in the online world, always think twice and verify before you click, share information, or respond to unsolicited requests. Stay alert, stay sceptical, and when in doubt, don't respond – it could save you from a world of trouble.

If you do encounter one of these attempts, don't hesitate to report it to the appropriate authorities or to a trusted adult who can help you navigate the situation. Make smart choices online, and encourage your friends to be just as cautious. Your digital security is in your hands, so take control and keep your information safe.

Design

Create a leaflet to explain one of these scams to an elderly person.

Remember to highlight examples to show how easy it is to fall for scammers tricks.

Microsoft's climbdown over its creepy Recall feature shows its AI strategy is far from intelligent

The tech company's new Windows machines can take constant screenshots of users' every action – quelle surprise, it's a privacy minefield.

By John Naughton

On 20 May, Yusuf Mehdi, a cove who rejoices in the magnificent title of executive vice-president, consumer chief marketing officer of Microsoft, launched its Copilot+ PCs, a 'new category' of Windows machines that are 'designed for AI'. They are, needless to say, 'the fastest, most intelligent Windows PCs ever built' and they will 'enable you to do things you can't on any other PC'.

What kinds of things? Well, how about generating and refining AI images in near real-time directly on the computer? Bridging language barriers by translating audio from 40-plus languages into English? Or enabling you to 'easily find and remember what you have seen in your PC'.

Eh? This remarkable memory prosthesis is called Recall. It takes constant screenshots in the background while you go about your daily computer business. Microsoft's Copilot+ machine-learning tech then scans (and 'reads') each of these screenshots in order to make a searchable database of every action performed on your computer and then stores it on the machine's disk. So not only will you be able to search for a website you had previously visited, but you can also search for a very specific thing that you read or saw on that site. That jacket you saw on a tab a few weeks ago but you simply cannot remember who was selling it. The AI, though, knows about jackets and can find it. But of course, this ability to remember extends to other apps on your machine: those full-text passwords you used when accessing your bank or logging into a paywalled site, for example. 'Recall is like bestowing a photographic memory on everyone who buys a Copilot+ PC,' Mehdi said. 'Anything you've ever seen or done, you'll now more or less be able to find.' What's not to like?

Lots, it turns out. The moment Recall emerged in preview mode, people were reminded of The Entire History of You from the first season of Black Mirror. It was about a hyper-modern, sci-fi society where everyone wears an implant that records everything they do, see and hear. (It doesn't end well.) Security experts were immediately more suspicious – especially when it was realised that Recall was on by default and needed a dive into Windows's settings to turn it off. The UK's Information Commissioner's Office said that it was 'having discussions with Microsoft' about Recall.

And Charlie Stross, the sci-fi author and tech critic, called it a privacy 'shit-show for any organisation that handles medical records or has a duty of legal confidentiality; indeed, for any business that has to comply with GDPR [general data protection regulation]'. He also said: 'Suddenly, every PC becomes a target for discovery during legal proceedings. Lawyers can subpoena your Recall database and search it, no longer being limited to email but being able to search for terms that came up in Teams or Slack or Signal messages, and potentially verbally via Zoom or Skype if speech-to-text is included in Recall data.'

The only good news for Microsoft is it seems to have belatedly acknowledged that Recall has been a fiasco.

Faced with this pushback, Microsoft stuck by its guns for 17 days but eventually, on 7 June, caved in, announcing that Recall would be made opt-in instead of on by default, and also introducing extra security precautions – only producing results from Recall after user authentication, for example, and never decrypting data stored by the tool until after a search query.

The only good news for Microsoft here is that it seems to have belatedly acknowledged that Recall has been a fiasco. The more interesting question, though, is what it reveals about the internal culture of the organisation. For decades, Microsoft has been a dull but dependable behemoth, secure in the knowledge that although it had initially fumbled the opportunities of the web – and, later, the smartphone – it had nevertheless retained in effect a monopoly in organisational computing. After all, almost every business and governmental organisation in the world runs on Windows software. The company belatedly got into the cloud computing business and its general counsel, Brad Smith, took on the role of the only adult in the tech fraternity house, issuing ponderous think pieces about ethics, corporate responsibility and other worthy topics.

And then came AI and ChatGPT, and Microsoft chief executive Satya Nadella's astonishing pre-emptive strike, investing $13bn in OpenAI, the maker of ChatGPT, to get a head start on the other tech companies – particularly Google – in the next big thing. What was most striking, though, was the way Nadella described what he was really up to: trying to make Google 'dance' is how he put it. The contrast with the ancien régime of Bill Gates and Steve Ballmer could not have been starker: they always sought to obliterate the opposition; Nadella merely wants to tease it. The subliminal message: Microsoft has been through its midlife crisis. It's no longer paranoid and is enjoying playing with its latest toy: AI. The message of the Recall fiasco, though, is that it isn't a toy. And it can blow up in your face.

6 July 2024

Are your devices spying on you?

We all want things in our life which save us time and make life just that bit easier. To satisfy that need, each year household and consumer technology becomes more and more advanced. Although the security in smart technology is improving, there's still a real risk of your everyday devices being exploited.

If you received any kind of smart device as a Christmas present or you're considering buying one yourself, hold onto your credit card for a moment. And keep reading to uncover some enlightening facts about the latest tech available.

Our experts at UK NACE (the UK National Authority for Counter-Eavesdropping) know all too well that smart and wearable technology is susceptible to malware attacks. They give us the lowdown and their tips for improving the safety of your smart devices.

Keep your devices up to date with the latest security

Devices such as smartphones and smart watches are constantly being updated with new security software. So, it's vital to ensure yours is always running the latest version. However, that alone won't stop hackers from trying to get unauthorised access to your personal information.

The older your device, the greater the risk of attack. This is especially the case when it's no longer supported by the manufacturer, as it won't receive any new security updates. This could potentially leave your device wide open to attacks, and your personal data vulnerable. Attackers aren't only focused on old devices though.

UK NACE say, 'There's a whole industry out there looking for brand new ways to target the most modern hardware. These kind of attacks are called 'zero-day' exploits and they typically take advantage of unknown vulnerabilities in new software or hardware, well before anyone realises anything is wrong!'

Beware fake updates

Attackers can also gain access to your technology through other methods – the most common is fake and harmful updates. Whether that's general software, security or specific app updates – their authenticity can be hard to distinguish from official sources.

Originators of fake updates commonly send out a pop-up ad or alert. This says your device is infected with malware and offers to scan your system, or asks you to click on a link to update the software.

For these to take effect, it requires you to update your permissions to allow apps to access your location, camera and contacts list. This helps attackers, advertisers and app developers profile your behaviour. It can also lead to you giving away your personal information.

Smartphones and smartwatches

Smartphones are the perfect eavesdropping device, or 'bugs'.

They're easily programmable and have constant power. Unlike many traditionally concealed eavesdropping devices,

this means you could potentially be tracked and listened to continuously.

Modern smartphones have features, such as cameras, microphones, GPS (Global Positioning System) and more. These all provide a variety of options for an attacker who is looking to exploit you. Whether that's to track you or gain access to your personal information, such as your address, bank details, passwords or pictures.

What about smartwatches? Smartwatches and fitness trackers present a different challenge to a hacker. But it is still possible to exploit these as eavesdropping devices, especially when linked to a smartphone. This can end up with you having more than just your steps being tracked!

If knowing your GPS location wasn't unsettling enough, an experienced attacker can use the motion and orientation senses in your device to calculate your ATM pin numbers and passwords.

Top tips to protect your personal data

To help prevent a malware attack on your smart devices, UK NACE strongly recommends regularly updating the security settings. This is particularly important, if you store a lot of your personal information on your smartphone for instance.

So, the next time you see a genuine new update pop up on your device, install it straight away. Don't leave the door open for attackers to profit from your data.

This also goes for when you get a new device. Before you begin to use it in earnest, check whether it's running the latest version of software and continue to do this regularly.

You should also keep your smart devices away from places where you're holding sensitive or classified conversations. This reduces the risk of someone eavesdropping on your in-person discussions. If in doubt, leave the device outside the room!

Need advice on how to counter these types of eavesdropping attacks better? Speak to UK NACE or your organisation's security adviser if you have one.

You can improve your device's security further by:

- re-setting your password every couple of months and using different passwords for each account or site you use – take a look at the National Cyber Security Centre guides on the use of password managers and two factor authentication
- updating your privacy settings – this is particularly important with your social media accounts
- using an anti-malware app on your device – these help protect you from attackers planting viruses within your technology.

5 January 2022

The smart devices harvesting your data

Smart devices may not be spying on you, but they are harvesting your data, according to a new consumer report from *Which?*

By Elizabeth Greenberg

'Is my smart speaker spying on me?'

It's a common enough concern that *Which?* investigated the data collection practices of popular household smart devices across the UK to find out if our smart devices are actually eavesdropping on us, or if it's just paranoia.

While smart devices may not be 'spying' on us in the traditional sense, a new consumer review from *Which?* shows that the data collection methods of top household device brands are arguably more intensive than they need to be.

Which? went through the data collection practices of multiple smart devices, ranging from speakers, to TVs, to washing machines, to analyse the data they collect.

Their findings show that while smart devices may not be spying on us, it is only because they don't really need to – the data they collect every day is enough to track our location, our economic status, and our consumption practices.

Below are the data practices of some of the most common smart devices in UK homes.

Smart speakers

While smart speakers are supposed to only listen to you when you specifically want them to, this doesn't mean that's the only time they collect data.

Which? found an interesting pattern concerning the data collection differences between consumers with smart speakers attached to an Android or Apple device.

Those using an Android device were typically asked to provide more data – Amazon Echo, Google Next, Bose, and Sonos requested precise and coarse location data on Android devices, where as Apple users were only asked this same data by Amazon Echo.

Further, *Which?* found that Bose's smart speakers share their user data with Meta.

Security cameras and doorbells

Google Nest appeared to ask for the most information out of all the security cameras and doorbells *Which?* investigated, asking for users' names, birth dates and addresses, email, and phone number.

For Android users, Amazon, Arlo, and Ezviz products wanted background location data, meaning that they could keep track of the user's location when they were not using the app.

Which? also found that Ezviz devices have the biggest number of active tracking firms, including Google, Meta, Huawei, and Pangle, TikTok's business marketing unit.

According to the consumer group, all the permissions among the cameras and doorbells are activated by default. While users can manually opt out, this requires settings changes that might compromise some working aspects of the device or its associated app.

Smart TVs

In order to keep track of what you watch, most smart TVs use a system called automatic content recognition (ACR) – this can track what you watch via an app, via traditional TV, or even though a DVD player or gaming device.

This is typically an option; however, some brands like LG, Sony, and Samsung bundle these permissions with other terms and conditions in an 'accept all' button.

Most brands offer tracking options that can be opt-in/opt-out, like personalised ads, usage history, location services, and voice recognition.

Which? did not find any smart TV brands that offered behaviour tracking by default, with these services requiring an opt-in and can be adjusted in the TV menu.

Smart washing machines

Which? said they were surprised by the amount of data tracking they identified from smart washing machines in the UK.

Every washing machine required users to create an account to use the smart settings – for LG and Hoover, users had to provide their date of birth to access the app.

Most washing machines requested location data of both Android and Apple users, and LG and Samsung even requested permission to access Photos from Apple users.

Miele went so far as to track users' precise location as a default and required setting to use the app.

As part of their research, *Which?* also investigated the practices of consumers concerning the terms and conditions of different smart devices, where the details on data collection would be contained.

The terms and conditions of all 23 brands they investigated totalled 199,905 words, which would take the average reader over 13 hours to get through. Google Nest's T&Cs total to a staggering 20,000 words, which still may not be comprehensible to the average consumer.

Data protection concerns

With companies wanting location data just to do laundry, it is no surprise that some consumers are growing more concerned around data protection.

In the UK, companies do have to rationalise why they collect certain data points, but these can often be listed under a vague category of the company's 'legitimate interest.'

'Consumers have already paid for smart products, in some cases thousands of pounds, so it is excessive that they have to continue to 'pay' with their personal information,' Rocio Concha, *Which?* director of policy and advocacy, said.

'Firms should not collect more data than they need to provide the service that's on offer, particularly if they are going to bury this important information in lengthy terms and conditions.

'The Information Commissioner's Office should crack down on data collection by manufacturers and marketing firms that appears to go beyond 'legitimate interests'. A proper standard or code of practice should also be put in place to make the rules clearer.'

In response, Stephen Almond, the executive director of regulatory risk at the Information Commissioner's Office said: 'People should be able to enjoy the benefits of using their connected devices without having excessive amounts of their personal data gathered. This simply isn't a price we expect to pay.

'To maintain trust in these products companies must be transparent about the data they collect and how they use it, and ensure that the data is not used or shared in ways that people would not expect. The ICO is developing guidance on data protection and Internet of Things devices and we will act where we don't see the rules being followed.'

11 September 2023

Alexa, who else is listening?

Your smart speaker is designed to listen, but could it be eavesdropping too?

By Jake Moore

Ever since Amazon came under fire for being able to potentially listen in on people through its Echo smart speakers, and even transcribe what they were saying, I have been intrigued by the idea of how IoT could be used to snoop on us, unbeknown to the victims. Big tech companies behind Alexa-enabled and other similar devices have since taken steps towards making them more privacy focused, but I recently demonstrated a feature that you should be aware of.

Let's cut right to the chase.

Trouble with an ex

I was recently asked by a friend to help check if she had been hacked, because she could not work out how her ex-partner knew specific information about her life and even private conversations she had had.

I first checked her phone and laptop by running ESET's security software, and couldn't see any malware or anything untoward. She mentioned that it was as if her conversations were being listened to and mentioned some of what she had only said to others had been relayed back verbatim.

This is when I checked for listening bugs. I didn't discover anything that shouldn't be there. However, I was interested in the family's Amazon Echo Dot smart speaker and asked who could have access to it. She told me that her ex-partner had set the device up two years previous, when they were together, and they both had access to the speaker via a shared account, but only she used it now.

As she hadn't changed her Amazon password – or any other account passwords – since her breakup with her partner, this was a good place to start investigating. I wondered if the device could be used to eavesdrop remotely via the app

by anyone with access to the account, which would have let them listen in to her conversations. I remembered I had heard it was possible, but I wanted to test myself that an Alexa device could be used as a covert listening device.

So I bought an Amazon Echo Dot and long story short, my gut feeling didn't fail me.

The privilege problem

Some smart devices can be taken out of the box and immediately plugged in and used with default – and therefore usually insecure – settings. Obviously I have never been a huge fan of default privacy and security settings on the majority of smart (or almost any other) devices even after Amazon and a number of other technology giants have been forced to improve their settings in order to better protect users from intrusive practices by manufacturers or third parties.

Now, people don't normally realise how easily the devices themselves could be used as spying tools by anyone (more precisely, the device's admin) with illicit intent. (Obviously it's not a security vulnerability if an admin can enable it via a checkbox – take note of Law #6 in Microsoft's Ten Immutable Laws of Security: 'A computer is only as secure as the administrator is trustworthy'.)

So, I set up my Echo Dot with a unique and strong password and enabled two-factor authentication using an authenticator app, and connected it to my phone. I was also able to connect it to my iPad with ease and I was relatively happy with the security.

I then went to 'Devices' in the app and selected my 'Echo Dot' and 'Settings', then enabled 'Communication'. I then tapped on the 'Drop In' feature to enable it. Then back in the

'Communicate' tab, all I had to do was select 'Drop In' and select my Echo Dot and I was able to listen in to the room that it was in. Easy as pie. I even logged off my home Wi-Fi and connected via 4G to prove I could easily do this from another remote location too.

When you Drop In and listen in to a room, the device light ring displays a spinning green light and it also makes a small ring sound to make those in the room aware of the Drop In. I was unable to Drop In with this light and sound turned off, but an unsuspecting victim might not hear it or simply think nothing of it. After all, these devices tend to make lots of sounds and always seem to have coloured light rings for some reasons.

I also decided to check the device logs via my app, but unfortunately there weren't any logs or anything to suggest I had 'dropped in', which makes forensic evidence more difficult in such a situation. Logs in Echo Dot devices are called 'Activity', but there's no way to record the use of the Drop In feature.

The spy in your smart speaker

Back to my friend now. When I asked her if there was a chance her Echo Dot could have been used to listen in, it seemed like she experienced a lightbulb moment. She noted that her Alexa would often have coloured rings spinning and she assumed the sounds were to do with her self-claimed 'deluge of Amazon purchases' and other notifications.

She claimed that she simply thought that her Alexa was listening for keywords, rather than allowing anyone with her password to listen in on her. She immediately felt uneasy,

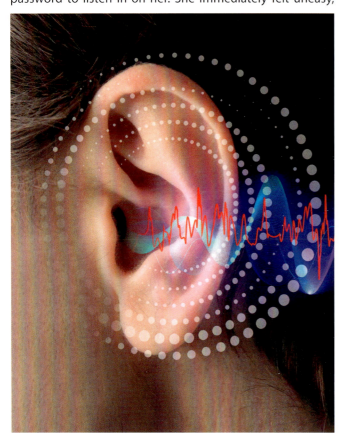

changed her password, and made her phone the only device pairable with her Echo Dot.

Her device has not made any strange sounds or lit up unintentionally since, and she says she now feels far safer.

Is your home bugged?

There are lots of listening devices on the market, but those hiding in plain sight (and not normally thought of as 'listening bugs') are often the most commonly used. It goes without saying that we should be aware of their capabilities if they are going to feature heavily in our homes.

As a result, it is vital that people follow a few tips when using smart technology to remain safe and secure:

- Always use strong and unique passwords
- Enable two-factor authentication
- Review the device's settings
- Only connect to devices that you own access to
- Do thorough account maintenance – configure user permissions and disable or remove accounts if they're not needed
- Change the password if you suspect someone has access to the account who shouldn't
- Turn off the device or disable listening mode when having sensitive conversations

iPhones as listening devices

Lastly, aside from the perhaps more obvious devices like smart speakers, did you know that Apple AirPods can also be used as listening devices? Few people seem to be aware that all that somebody has to do is turn on an accessibility feature called Live Listen on their iPhone and with AirPods in their ears, they can use the phone, left in any room, as a listening device. Who would suspect that an apparently 'forgotten' phone was actually a deliberately planted 'bug'?

Stay safe!

11 July 2023

The above information is reprinted with kind permission from Jake Moore.
© 2024 Jake Moore

www.jakemoore.uk

Yes, it sounds like a conspiracy theory. But maybe our phones really are listening to us

Big brands already know far too much about us. But Cox Media Group's 'Active Listening' software adds a whole new layer of creepiness.

By Arwa Mahdawi

Conspiracy theorists of the world, rip off that tinfoil hat and take a bow: you were (kinda) right. Despite the fact pretty much everyone has a story involving chatting about something only to see an ad for that something pop up on a device, the idea that your phone actively listens to you has long been dismissed as silly. After all, brands don't need to eavesdrop like that – they already have access to millions of data points that build up a detailed picture of your habits and predicted purchases.

But just because brands don't need to listen to your conversations, it doesn't mean that there aren't companies figuring out creepy new ways to mine your data. 404 Media, a tech-focused news site, recently got hold of a pitch deck from Cox Media Group (CMG), touting its 'Active Listening' software, which targets adverts based on what people say near their device microphones. The presentation doesn't specify whether this voice data comes from smart TVs, smart speakers, or smartphones but the slide where it extols 'the power of voice (and our devices' microphones)' has a picture of people looking at their phones.

I'm not going to make the predictable *Black Mirror* reference because CMG already has. When 404 Media reported on Active Listening last year, CMG's website had the following (now deleted) blurb: 'What would it mean … if you could target potential clients who are actively discussing their need for your services in their day-to-day conversations? No, it's not a *Black Mirror* episode – it's Voice Data.'

It's hard to know how widespread the use of this service is, but CMG's deck lists Facebook, Google and Amazon among its partners – though this doesn't necessarily mean they've partnered on this particular technology. Amazon, for its part, has said it has never worked with CMG, and Google removed CMG from its Partners Program after the 404 report. Meta, Facebook's parent company, said it is investigating whether CMG has violated its terms of service. While a lot of details remain murky, what's clear is this: privacy died a long time ago. Nothing is off-limits for some advertisers – there have even been experiments with 'targeted dream incubation' in an attempt to brand your dreams. The future is a meticulously personalised, highly targeted nightmare.

4 September 2024

What is GDPR

In a world where we constantly share information online – chatting with friends, posting photos on social media, or buying the latest gadgets – our personal data seems to fly around the digital universe at the speed of light. With all this sharing, you might wonder: 'Is my information safe?' That's where GDPR comes in, and here's what you need to know about it.

GDPR, or the General Data Protection Regulation, is a bit like a superhero for your personal data. It's a set of rules that came into effect on 25 May 2018 across the European Union (EU), which includes the UK for the time being. These laws give you more control over your personal information and how it's used by companies, organisations, or even your school.

So, what counts as personal data? It could be anything that identifies you, like your name, photos, email address, and even the IP address of your computer or phone. GDPR protects this data so that it's not misused in ways you wouldn't want.

Here are the superpowers GDPR gives you:

- **Right to Information:** You have the right to know exactly what information companies have about you and why they want it.

- **Right to Access:** Ever curious about what info a company has on you? Under GDPR, you can ask for a copy of your personal data.

- **Right to Rectification:** Found a mistake in your data? Maybe a wrong address or a misspelt name? You can have it corrected.

- **Right to Erasure:** Also known as the 'right to be forgotten,' this allows you to ask companies to delete your personal data when it's no longer needed.

- **Right to Restrict Processing:** If you're not sure about how your data is being used or its accuracy, you can pause its use until everything's cleared up.

- **Right to Data Portability:** This one's pretty cool. It means you can take your data from one service provider to another. So, if you're switching social media platforms, you can take all your photos and posts with you.

- **Right to Object:** You can say no to the use of your data for things like marketing. Don't want to be bombarded with ads? This is your go-to right.

- **Rights in relation to automated decision-making and profiling:** You can challenge decisions made without human involvement, like computer-generated choices affecting your education or job opportunities.

Why should you care?

Well, it's all about respecting your privacy and making sure you stay in the driver's seat when it comes to your data. Companies now have to work harder to protect your information and can't be careless with it. If they are, they could face massive fines, so it's in their best interest to keep your data safe.

What's in it for businesses?

GDPR isn't just about setting up boundaries; it's also about building trust. Companies that follow these rules can improve their relationship with customers. When you trust a company with your data, you're more likely to use their services.

What can you do?

Stay informed and exercise your rights. Always read the privacy policies (we know, they can be a bore) to understand how your data is being used. And if you feel like your data isn't being handled properly, speak up! GDPR has given you the voice to do so.

The bottom line is that GDPR is an essential step towards data protection in the age we live in. By knowing your rights, you can make sure that your data doesn't end up in the wrong hands or used in ways you wouldn't approve of. Empower yourself with knowledge, and take control of your digital footprint.

What are cookies on websites?

Everyone has seen or heard of internet cookies, but what exactly are cookies, and why are they important? In this digital age, cookies play a crucial role in enhancing the user experience and enabling the smooth operation of websites. This article will demystify cookies, explaining their purpose, types, and implications for privacy.

Understanding Cookies

Cookies are small text files stored on a user's device by a web browser when they visit a website. These files contain data specific to the user's interactions with the site, such as login details, preferences, and tracking information. When the user revisits the site, the browser returns the cookies to the server, allowing the site to remember previous activities and settings.

Types of Cookies

Session cookies: These cookies are temporary and are deleted once the user closes the browser. They help maintain user sessions, enabling actions like adding items to a shopping cart or staying logged in during a single browsing session.

Persistent cookies: Unlike session cookies, persistent cookies remain on the user's device for a specified period or until manually deleted. They are used to remember login credentials, language preferences, and other settings for future visits.

First-party Ccookies: These cookies are set by the website the user visits. They are primarily used to enhance user experience by remembering preferences and providing personalised content.

Third-party cookies: Set by domains other than the one the user is visiting, these cookies are often used for tracking and advertising purposes. For example, ad networks use third-party cookies to deliver targeted ads based on a user's browsing history across different sites.

The role of cookies

Cookies serve several essential functions, including:

Personalisation: Cookies enable websites to remember user preferences, such as language settings and themes, ensuring a consistent and tailored experience.

Authentication: They facilitate the login process by remembering credentials, reducing the need for users to re-enter their information on subsequent visits.

Tracking and analytics: Cookies help website owners track user behaviour, gather analytics data, and improve site performance. This information is valuable for optimising content and enhancing user engagement.

Advertising: Cookies support targeted advertising by tracking user behaviour across different websites. Advertisers can deliver personalised ads based on the user's interests and browsing history.

Privacy concerns and management

While cookies offer numerous benefits, they also raise privacy concerns. Tracking cookies, particularly third-party ones, can collect extensive data about users' online activities, leading to potential privacy breaches and unwanted targeted advertising.

To address these concerns, many countries have implemented regulations, such as the General Data Protection Regulation (GDPR) in the European Union, which requires websites to obtain user consent before storing non-essential cookies. Users can also manage cookies through browser settings, allowing them to delete existing cookies or block new ones from being set.

Managing cookies

Most modern browsers provide options for managing cookies. Users can:

- View and delete cookies: Browsers offer tools to view the cookies stored on the device and delete them as needed.

- Block cookies: Users can configure browser settings to block all cookies or only third-party cookies, enhancing privacy at the expense of some website functionality.

- Private browsing: This mode ensures that cookies are not stored once the browsing session ends, offering a more private browsing experience.

Cookies are integral to the modern web, enhancing user experience and enabling various functionalities. However, they also pose privacy challenges that require careful management. By understanding what cookies are and how they work, users can make informed decisions about online privacy and enjoy a more personalised and secure web experience.

23 July 2024

Control of your images online

A picture is worth a thousand words – so the saying goes.

Billions of photographs are uploaded to the internet every day. Social media use is on the rise, so more images are being posted.

People like to share photos of themselves, their friends and things that they do.

But who owns the images you post? What can you do if someone posts images of you that you don't want them to post?

Copyright of images

Photos are usually protected by copyright as they are thought of as artistic works. Copyright happens automatically in the UK when a photograph is created, as long as it meets the needed criteria for copyright protection. This means the person who took the photo usually owns it. The copyright of images usually lasts for the life of the creator plus 70 years from the end of the year of their death.

There are times when this is not the case. For example if a photo was taken by someone as part of their job. Then the employer would usually own the copyright for the photo. But there might be an agreement in place to say otherwise.

The owner of the copyright can also transfer ownership or licence the copyright to other people. Then the original photographer may no longer be the owner of the copyright.

If anyone wants to use a photo that someone else owns copyright for, they need to have the permission of the person who owns it. This includes posting it online.

If you think someone has been using a photo you own the copyright to without your permission, you could contact them. You could let them know that you own the copyright and you would like them to take it down. If they do not agree to this, you could ask the website operator where your photo has been posted to take it down. If this also doesn't work, you could think about taking legal action for copyright infringement. Copyright laws can be complicated. For example when they relate to older photographs taken when the law was different. You should speak to a legal adviser if you need help.

Ownership after you upload

Ownership doesn't change once an image is uploaded to the internet. But the rights to use it might change.

For example, if you post a photo (that you took) on a social media site like Facebook, you will still own it, but you'll be agreeing to the site's terms and conditions. These may give the website operators a licence to use copyright photos. This means the site could use, copy or edit your photo for different things without you knowing. You should always check the website's terms and conditions before you upload photos if you are worried about your photos being used without your knowledge.

Other people may also be able to share any posts you upload with your photo without your knowledge or telling them they can.

Publishing images of you without your consent

As images are shared more and more, there is a good chance that a picture of you could be posted without your consent or knowledge.

If you took the photo, you usually own it. But, if you didn't take the photo but you are in it, someone could breach your rights (such as data protection or privacy rights) by posting it. This can be true even if you do not own the copyright to it. If your rights have been breached will depend on how the photo has been used. It will depend on whether the person posting the photo had a legal basis to do so. If you don't know if your rights have been breached, you should speak to a legal adviser. Things that may be considered are:

* if the photo was taken in public or on private property
* who took the photo
* if there are children in the photo
* what is happening in the photo.

If someone has posted a photo of you that you do not want to be shared, you can ask the poster to take it down. If they don't agree to take it down, you could think about speaking to a legal adviser. You could also try using mediation to try and fix the issue.

You could also ask the social media site where the photo is posted to take it down. If the social media site will not take it down either, you could think about speaking to a legal adviser. They can tell you what legal steps you can take to have the photo taken down. This may change depending on the situation.

Revenge porn

'Revenge porn' is unfortunately happening more and more often. This is when someone shares an intimate sexual photo or film of someone else without their permission. This is intended to cause them distress.

It could be shared on the internet, by text message or in person.

Revenge porn is a crime. Victims should call the police on 101. It is important to keep any evidence, such as messages, images and screenshots.

Help is available from a legal adviser. Support is also available from the Revenge Porn Helpline and Victim Support. You can call Victim Support free on 0808 168 9111.

The above information is reprinted with kind permission from Legal Choices.

© 2024 Legal Choices

www.legalchoices.org.uk

Is the UK the most surveilled country?

In a world where technology is constantly evolving, concerns about privacy and surveillance are becoming more common. You might have heard that the UK is one of the most surveilled countries in the world, but is that true? Let's take a closer look.

CCTV everywhere

One of the first things people think of when they talk about surveillance in the UK is the sheer number of CCTV cameras. In fact, it's estimated that there are around 7.5 million CCTV cameras across the country. To put that into perspective, that's about one camera for every 11 people. These cameras are in public spaces like streets, parks, and transport stations, but also in private businesses like shops, offices, and schools.

CCTV is often seen as a way to prevent crime, as it allows authorities to monitor public areas and respond to incidents more quickly. It also helps in investigations, as footage can be used to catch criminals after a crime has been committed. However, not everyone feels comfortable knowing they're being watched so frequently. Some people believe it's a breach of privacy, and they worry about who has access to all that footage.

Online surveillance

Cameras aren't the only form of surveillance in the UK. There's also a lot of focus on what happens online. In 2016, the UK government passed the Investigatory Powers Act, nicknamed the 'Snooper's Charter.' This law gives security services and government agencies the power to collect and store data from people's online activities, including browsing history and communications.

This is a big concern for people who value their privacy, especially in the age of smartphones and social media. Every time you use an app, post on Instagram, or send a message, data is being collected, and with laws like the Snooper's Charter, some of that data can be accessed by the

Government. The argument for this level of surveillance is that it helps prevent terrorism and serious crimes, but critics argue that it's a slippery slope towards a 'Big Brother' society.

How does the UK compare?

While the UK has a lot of surveillance, it's not necessarily the most surveilled country in the world. China, for example, has far more CCTV cameras – around 540 million – as part of its extensive surveillance system, which is much more invasive than in the UK. In China, surveillance is often paired with facial recognition technology, and people can be tracked in real-time based on their movements and even their social behaviour.

The US is also heavily surveilled, particularly through online data collection by both the government and private companies. However, the level of physical surveillance, like CCTV, is generally lower than in the UK.

What does it mean for you?

The amount of surveillance in the UK raises important questions about privacy and safety. On the one hand, surveillance can make public spaces safer and help solve crimes. On the other hand, it can feel like a violation of personal privacy, and there's always the risk of data being misused.

As technology continues to advance, it's important to stay informed about how surveillance works and what your rights are. Being aware of these issues will help you understand the balance between security and privacy and decide where you stand on this debate.

So, is the UK the most surveilled country? Not quite, but it's definitely one of the most watched, both on the streets and online. The key question is whether that makes you feel safer or more uneasy.

Who's watching: the cities with the most CCTV cameras

In a world where surveillance is ever increasing, where are the most CCTV cameras?

By the end of 2021, an estimated one billion surveillance cameras were in operation globally; 54% of them are located in China. Chinese cities are under the heaviest CCTV surveillance in the world, but there's growing concern about the surveillance tactics, and lack of data protection, in several countries. No single country is consistent in protecting the privacy of its citizens and only five have 'adequate safeguards' in place (Ireland, France, Portugal, Denmark and Norway). Here we present the cities with the highest number of public CCTV cameras per person in the world. These cameras are used by government entities, such as law enforcement, across public locations that include buildings and transport.

Cities with the most CCTV per people

1. Cities of China – 373 cameras per 1,000 people (estimate)

Data privacy laws: Extensive surveillance

It's difficult to know how many cameras are installed in any Chinese city; one conservative estimate by IHS Markit puts the number at 540 million cameras countrywide – more than one camera per three people. China's technology goes beyond facial recognition to 'emotion recognition', touted as a way to predict problematic behaviour in prisons, workplaces, schools and care homes.

2. Indore, India – 62.52 cameras

Data privacy laws: Systemic failure to maintain safeguards

3. Hyderabad, India – 41.8 cameras

4. Dehli, India – 26.7 cameras

5. Chennai, India – 24.53 cameras

6. Singapore, Singapore – 18.04 cameras

Data privacy laws: Some safeguards/weakened protection

Singapore is the world's leading 'smart city' – a city that uses data collected from a range of sources such as social media, sensors and CCTV cameras to make its facilities and services more efficient and to enhance its citizens' quality of life. The ubiquitous use of CCTV by its Smart Nation initiative has reportedly helped to reduce traffic congestion, littering and vandalism, and has successfully located criminals using facial recognition technology. State surveillance is often justified by its potential to reduce crime, but while Singapore's crime rates are some of the lowest in the world, it's difficult to determine whether this comes as a result of its extensive CCTV network or its harsh criminal penalties for everything from chewing gum to drug trafficking – the country is estimated to have the highest execution rate in the world relative to its population.

7. Moscow, Russia – 16.85 cameras

Data privacy laws: Systemic failure to maintain safeguards

8. Baghdad, Iraq – 15.97 cameras

9. St Petersburg, Russia – 12.65 cameras

10. London, England – 13.35 cameras

Data privacy laws: Some safeguards/weakened protection

11. Los Angeles, USA – 8.77 cameras

Data privacy laws: Some safeguards/weakened protection

12. Uganda – 0.64 cameras

Almost 80% of countries have some government use of facial recognition technology. Uganda doesn't feature among the countries with the highest number of CCTV cameras, with only 0.64 cameras per 1,000 people, but alongside China and Myanmar, its government's use of facial recognition technology is among the most invasive. In 2019, it was confirmed that Huawei was installing surveillance equipment in cities throughout Uganda – the same year the Chinese tech giant was revealed to have helped the Ugandan government spy on its political opponents. This CCTV system is part of Huawei's Safe City project, which has been launched in cities across at least 52 countries. Huawei has also provided training on 'critical incident management' to the Ugandan police force, which plans to integrate data from its CCTV systems with other government agencies.

7 March 2023

The Met is watching you

We are passively accepting the development of a society of hyper-surveillance.

By Rosie Norman

Walking down my local high-street recently, I noticed several unmarked police vans. At first I was reassured by their presence since London has become something of a hotspot for violent crime lately. However, the Met Police were in fact not doing ordinary policing. Instead, they were trying out live facial recognition technology on the unsuspecting public (as a small sticker on the side of the van and a quick Google later revealed).

Although welcomed by some, it is clear that rapid technological advances haven't all been rainbows and unicorns. While people are beginning to recognise the fact that technology has had a grave effect on children's and young people's mental health, less well understood are the practical implications of rapid digitalisation.

One new statistic published by Parliament in a report on digital technologies estimates that by 2030 30% of UK jobs will be vulnerable to automation by AI and robotics. We also have to consider the ever-encroaching presence of technology in public life. A quick trip to the local supermarket will see you being followed by CCTV cameras your entire way around the shop, the dénouement of which is watching your pale and perhaps slightly sweaty mug as you scan through discounted Baked Beans and several Dairy Milks.

Yet even though 'live facial recognition technology' sounds almost laughably Orwellian, given that much of 1984 is concerned with living under constant monitoring and surveillance, the Met Police has in fact been using facial recognition technology since 2016.

Mobile units fitted with live facial recognition cameras allow the police to monitor, categorise and track us. This, they tell us, is so that they will be able to improve on their ability to catch perpetrators and prevent crime.

Live facial recognition cameras work by creating a biometric scan of your face to create a 'faceprint'. These faceprints contain sensitive data which, in theory, specifically identify you, much like a fingerprint. In other words, the software analyses a live video feed as the police cameras scan the faces of passers-by, comparing them against a watch list in real time.

Worryingly, according to the Met's own data, the technology misidentifies people a staggering 85% of the time. Furthermore, as Big Brother Watch points out, the Met's own report into the technology has shown the algorithm to have a racial bias, discriminating against women and people of colour. Big Brother Watch also estimates that so far over 3,000 people have been wrongly identified by police facial recognition technology.

Despite this, the Met and South Wales Police have been continuing to use this technology to scan thousands of innocent people in order to build up a database of images. In the last five years alone, over 5 million people's photographs have been uploaded to the police database without the consent of the individuals themselves.

Concerningly, there is currently no law governing facial recognition in the UK. The police are thus getting away with using this technology on the public by operating in a legal grey area. And while the EU has recently implemented laws to ban the use of live facial recognition technology in public spaces, the UK government has instead announced a £230 million budget for the expansion of live facial recognition technology.

Facial recognition technology is not just being used by the police and supermarkets, however. Clothes shops, galleries, music venues and bars have all been found to use surveillance.

In creating such a society, we would be handing state institutions tremendous power.

We are in very real danger of having our right to privacy taken from us without our consent. But is this something we really want? Would we actually prefer to live in a society where not just our every transaction, but our every move is monitored? In creating such a society, we would be handing state institutions tremendous power. How much faith do you have that it will not be misused? In the aftermath of the pandemic, it would be naive to feel at all secure.

Britain is already one of the most surveilled countries in the world. Proportionate to the population, we have as many CCTV cameras in Britain as there are in China. The next step is installing facial recognition technology in fixed cameras, something the Government is already planning to do. Imagine the potential of such technology if coupled with the Scottish Hate Crime and Public Order Act.

We need to think carefully now about whether we want to live in a country in which our every move is tracked, and all our behaviour is monitored. We need to look closely at China and other hyper-surveillance countries and decide whether that is the direction we want to go in.

In the meantime, the attempt by the already under-resourced police to cover up their failings by digitalising law and order is clearly something that needs to be taken more seriously than it is. Of course, we all want the police to be able to apprehend criminals – but sacrificing our privacy is a cost that must be weighed against the benefits. Besides, attempting to apprehend criminals after the fact is not as valuable as ensuring that crimes do not take place to begin with. Hyper-surveillance is a sticking plaster pressed across the cracks in our civilisation.

22 April 2024

Facial recognition

Facial recognition technology is being used by police and private companies in publicly accessible places. It breaches everyone's human rights, discriminates against people of colour and is unlawful. It's time to ban it.

What's happening?

Several police forces have used live facial recognition surveillance technology in public spaces since 2015, scanning millions of people's faces.

In 2020, Liberty client Ed Bridges won the world's first legal challenge to police use of the tech. The Court said South Wales Police's use of intrusive and discriminatory facial recognition violates privacy rights and breaks data protection and equality laws.

But despite the court ruling, several police forces have reaffirmed their commitment to it and are looking for ways around our court win. Private companies are also using the tech in publicly accessible places like shopping centres and train stations.

What is facial recognition?

Facial recognition works by matching the faces of people walking past special cameras to images of people on a watch list. It does this by scanning the distinct points of our faces and creating biometric maps – more like fingerprints than photographs.

Everyone in range is scanned and has their biometric data (their unique facial measurements) snatched without their consent.

The watch lists can contain pictures of anyone, including people who are not suspected of any wrongdoing, and the images can come from anywhere – even from our social media accounts.

South Wales Police and the Metropolitan Police have been using live facial recognition in public for years with no public or parliamentary debate.

They've used it on tens of thousands of us, everywhere from protests and football matches to music festivals, and even just busy streets.

Some private companies have also used the tech in publicly accessible places including King's Cross in London, and the Trafford Centre in Manchester.

Why should we be concerned?

Our court victory against South Wales Police shows that the lack of safeguards over whose image is included on a watch list violates everyone's right to privacy.

The Court also said the level of discretion officers have when choosing where to use the tech contributes to a breach of privacy rights.

But the Metropolitan Police, has confirmed its intention to continue using the tech despite admitting to just deploying it in busy areas where it can scan as many people as possible, and previously using it to track people experiencing mental health crises who were not wanted by the police.

Other police forces will follow the Met if facial recognition use is not stopped for good.

And history tells us that surveillance tech will always be disproportionately used against communities of colour. While facial recognition is known to misidentify black people – meaning if you are black you are more likely to be stopped, questioned and searched by police. The Metropolitan Police has often used it in ethnically diverse areas and at events likely to be highly attended by people of colour, including Notting Hill Carnival for two years running.

What are we calling for?

Creating law to govern police and private company use of facial recognition technology will not solve the human rights concerns or the tech's in-built discrimination.

And making the tech more accurate, meaning we could all be identified and tracked in real time, can never be viewed as the solution – especially as police will disproportionately use it against communities of colour.

The only solution is to ban it.

> **The police are supposed to protect us and make us feel safe – but I think the technology is intimidating and intrusive.**
>
> – Liberty client Ed Bridges

The above information is reprinted with kind permission from Liberty.

© 2024 Liberty (The National Council for Civil Liberties)

www.libertyhumanrights.org.uk

Five reasons why facial recognition must be banned

Mass surveillance tool is discriminatory, intrusive and oppressive. It needs to be banned.

1. It's discriminatory

Facial recognition technology is meant to identify people on a watchlist, but it's worse at recognising people of colour. This means black people and other people of colour are more likely to be stopped due to a false match.

This replicates discrimination seen throughout UK policing.

Even if the technology were improved to stop this from happening, it would nevertheless become a tool to enhance surveillance of already over-policed communities.

Police are already using it in areas with large ethnic minority populations and have used it at Notting Hill Carnival.

'When we know we're being watched, we change our behaviour'

2. It destroys our privacy

Recent polling commissioned by Liberty found 83% of us say our privacy is important. Facial recognition threatens to destroy this. It goes far beyond CCTV and can be used to track and monitor us. It can identify anyone on a watchlist, whenever they go in view of a camera – and there are no restrictions on who can be on a watchlist.

All of us should feel able to go about our lives privately – this is our right. Mass use of facial recognition in public would destroy that forever.

3. It undermines our freedom of expression

When we know we're being watched, we change our behaviour – in effect, we censor ourselves. We shouldn't have to face the prospect of being watched and monitored to go where we want, whether that be to walk down the high street, to see friends or to attend a political event or protest.

Even the threat of enhanced surveillance (combined with an incredibly broad definition of 'extremism') threatens our right to free expression.

Mass surveillance doesn't keep our society safe. Instead, it undermines the very rights and freedoms that allow us to stand up to power.

IBM, Amazon and Microsoft all halted their supply of facial recognition to police forces, citing fears over privacy, discrimination and potential racial profiling.

4. It's spreading

South Wales Police continue to 'pilot' facial recognition, which in reality amounts to operational use (they've used it 70 times), while the Metropolitan Police rolled it out in full earlier this year. Some police are even putting it on their smartphones so they can scan us wherever and whenever they choose.

Private companies are identifying and tracking people at shopping centres, football stadiums, museums, conference centres, shops and train stations.

It could soon be everywhere, fundamentally altering society and creating an oppressive mass surveillance state.

5. It's oppressive by design

In recent weeks, responding to pressure from racial justice campaigners, tech giants IBM, Amazon and Microsoft all halted their supply of facial recognition to police forces, citing fears over privacy, discrimination and potential racial profiling.

But they are asking for a moratorium so laws can be created to regulate the technology.

Introducing laws to regulate the use of facial recognition will not address the fundamental threats this tech poses. Its very design undermines our rights.

19 June 2020

Big tech firms profit from disorder. Don't let them use these riots to push for more surveillance

Live facial recognition can seem like a solution to criminality. But it magnifies injustice, and violates our civil liberties.

By Shami Chakrabarti

Far-right riots may not be the calmest moment for a reasoned debate about the regulation of big tech, but the eruption of racist violence in England and Northern Ireland raises urgent questions about the responsibilities of social media companies, and how the police use facial recognition technology. While social media isn't the root of these riots, it has allowed inflammatory content to spread like wildfire and helped rioters coordinate. Keir Starmer has pledged to address online impunity and increase the use of live facial recognition technology. We should applaud the former but be very wary of the latter idea.

Both technologies have profound implications for democratic accountability. Take social media. We are used to the adage that what's illegal in the real world is illegal in the virtual universe too. But in practice, years of cuts to the justice system have left it ill equipped to deal with the growth in racist and inflammatory content online. Explicit violent threats, and incitements to violence, have gone unpoliced, and dangerous and deliberate misinformation has spread. Both can be weapons used by hostile actors, including enemy states.

The great elephant in the room is the wealth, power and arrogance of the big tech emperors. Silicon Valley billionaires are richer than many countries. Some believe they can buy current and recently retired politicians, and see themselves as above both democracy and the law. That mature modern states should allow them unfettered freedom to regulate the content they monetise is a gross abdication of duty, given their vast financial interest in monetising insecurity and division. Is Elon Musk the legitimate arbiter of whether Mr Yaxley-Lennon's social media broadcasts are a threat to public order and security in the UK or anywhere else? Isn't it time we had judicial processes that would allow for the removal of particular material and the proportionate blocking of certain users?

Similar questions arise at the sharp end of law enforcement around the use of facial recognition. In recent years, this technology has been used on our streets without any significant public debate or any parliamentary authorisation. We wouldn't dream of allowing telephone taps, DNA retention or even stop and search and arrest powers to be so unregulated by the law, yet this is precisely what has

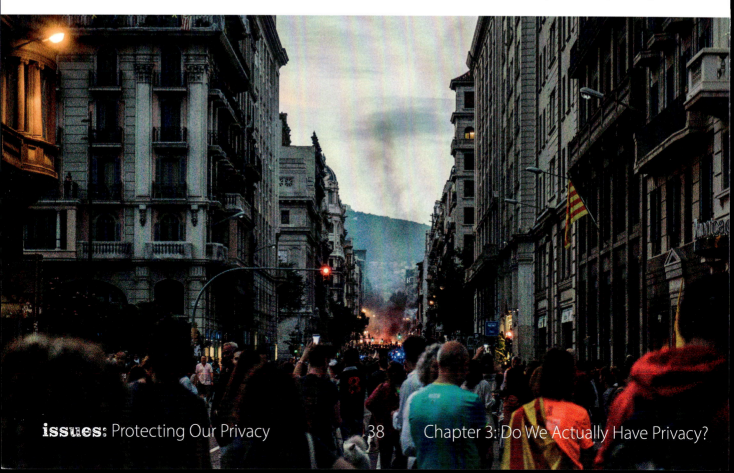

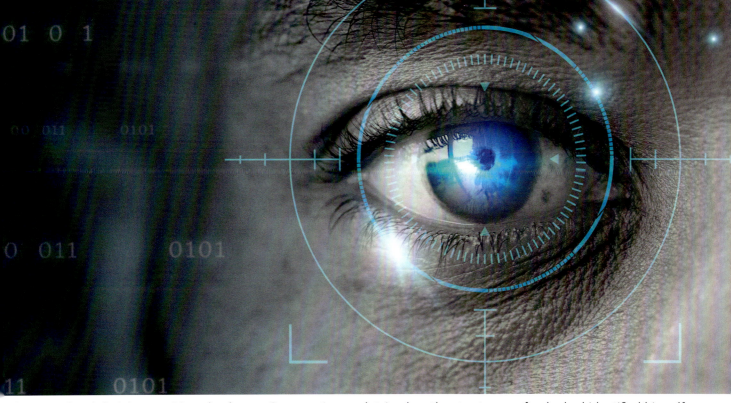

happened with facial recognition, thanks to a Conservative government that was casual with both the law and the doling out of public money to private contractors.

Our facial images are gathered en masse via CCTV cameras, the passport database and the internet. At no point were we asked about this, nor is there any statutory legal basis for it. People are placed on 'watchlists' with no statutory criteria. These lists typically include victims and vulnerable people alongside 'people of interest' and convicted criminals. Individual police forces have entered into direct contracts with private companies of their choosing, making opaque arrangements to trade our highly sensitive personal data with private companies that use it to develop proprietary technology. And there is no specific law governing how the police, or private companies such as retailers, are authorised to use this technology.

Facial recognition is incredibly intrusive and capable of achieving complete societal surveillance. It can also create significant injustice, particularly when it's deployed in real time as opposed to after a crime is captured on camera. Live facial recognition depends on cameras situated in public places that capture everyone who passes by. This increases the risk of false positive matches, where members of the public are incorrectly identified and flagged to police or security staff. Unless that person can then persuade an officer that they're not the person on the list, they risk facing an intrusive stop and search, or even an arrest.

This poses a huge threat to everyone's civil liberties, but there are further concerns about racial bias. Experts at Big Brother Watch believe the inaccuracy rate for live facial recognition since the police began using it is around 74%, and there are many cases pending about false positive IDs. One involved a black youth worker who was subject to a false match and detained on the street even after he had identified himself to the police. Another involved a teenager (who was also black) who was subject to a search and ejected from a shop after being told that she had been banned. Again, the shop's facial recognition camera misidentified her. As the post office operators will testify, such are the human dangers of believing in the infallibility of the machine.

In Europe the AI act, which came into force in the EU on 1 August, bans the use of live facial recognition in anything but extreme circumstances (such as an imminent terrorist threat). Why doesn't the UK have something similar? If we want to lead the world in exciting new technologies, we must surely seek to regulate them as our international partners do. The police and the Government have so far been silent on this legal black hole.

When corporate lobbyists descend on Liverpool for the first party conference of a new Labour government this September, ministers must not be deterred from making big tech more fairly accountable. Nor should companies be given yet more unaccountable contracts for intrusive technology that replaces legal code with opaque computer code. Total societal surveillance is a dangerous and poor substitute for intelligence-led community cooperation and policing. VIP lanes and cosy chats with billionaires at Bletchley Park must be replaced by parliamentary process and primary legislation. Not only would this protect our liberties under the law, but it could also go some way towards rebuilding people's trust in politics.

7 August 2024

Facial recognition cameras in supermarkets 'targeted at poor areas' in England

Southern Co-op chain more likely to install tech 'in deprived districts', says privacy rights group.

By Shanti Das, Home Affairs Correspondent

Facial recognition cameras installed by a supermarket chain to tackle shoplifting disproportionately target people in poorer areas, according to a privacy rights group.

Southern Co-op, which uses Facewatch live recognition cameras in 34 branches, typically has shops in richer-than-average neighbourhoods. But just five of the stores in which it uses Facewatch are in the richest third of neighbourhoods in England, while 14 are in the poorest.

Professor Pete Fussey, director of the Centre for Research into Information, Surveillance and Privacy at University of Essex, said the findings raised concerns about the targeting of people on the 'margins of society'. 'This is another example of the many ways in which surveillance is more intensely focused on minorities and those who are disadvantaged socioeconomically,' he said.

Southern Co-op, which is separate from the national Co-op chain, said it did not consider how deprived an area was, or other demographic information, when deploying the technology. The cameras were in locations considered high-risk based on 'our crime data and stock loss reports'.

Fussey said police and businesses often claimed decisions on where to use facial recognition were an 'objective judgment' based on crime levels. 'But the issue is that it's not clear at all,' he said. 'We're going to find crime in the areas we look at most heavily. And we look most heavily at suspect populations, those who are seen as threatening or outsiders, and the urban poor.'

Analysis by the privacy group Big Brother Watch used data supplied by Southern Co-op cross-referenced with the England-wide 2019 Indices of Multiple Deprivation. The index ranks more than 30,000 neighbourhoods across seven areas, including income and employment, to calculate their relative deprivation – with the number one ranked neighbourhood being the most deprived.

An average Southern Co-op store is in an area ranking at 19,835 out of 32,844, putting it in the best-off third of neighbourhoods. But supermarkets where facial recognition is deployed are in neighbourhoods ranked at 14,453 on average, placing them in the most deprived half.

Jake Hurfurt, the head of research at Big Brother Watch, said: 'This data shows that AI supermarket surveillance is being directed at poorer communities, who are more likely to suffer excessive invasions of their privacy and unfair treatment as a result.'

Increasingly used by police and private firms, live facial recognition operates in real-time to compare camera feeds with faces on a predetermined watchlist, to identify people of interest. Each time a match is found, the system generates an alert.

Advocates including police chiefs and the Government say the technology deters crime and helps identify offenders. But concerns have been raised over a lack of oversight and transparency as its use becomes more mainstream.

On Friday, the House of Lords Justice and Home Affairs committee wrote to the home secretary, James Cleverly, calling on him to urgently address concerns about live facial recognition use by police, which it said lacked 'clear legal foundation'.

The committee said there were 'no rigorous standards or systems of regulation' in place for monitoring the technology's use and 'no consistency in approaches to training' among police forces. 'The committee accepts that live facial recognition may be a valuable tool in apprehending criminals, but it is deeply concerned that its use is being expanded without proper scrutiny and accountability,' it said.

Fussey described use of the technology in Britain as a 'wild west'. 'There is no proper, robust, meaningful regulation of it. There's even less in the private sector than there is in the public sector,' he said.

Nick Fisher, the chief executive of Facewatch, said the technology was used to protect stock and staff and to deter crime. 'Retailers across the UK use Facewatch in those stores where it is necessary to do so because other crime prevention methods have been tried and failed,' he said. 'Their lawful use of Facewatch reduces crime between 30% and 70% in every location it is deployed in.'

A Southern Co-op spokesperson said its use of the technology was 'limited and targeted', and had helped cut crime. It recorded 38,262 incidents in 2022, including 'shoplifting, violence and physical and verbal abuse'. Internal figures showed a 34% reduction in violence against staff in 2021 compared with 2020 at shops using the technology. It acknowledged that this was due to 'a range of measures we are using to tackle crime, as well as a number of external factors'.

The spokesperson added that Southern Co-op did not maintain a 'watchlist' but its facial recognition provider had 'lists of individuals of interest who are known and evidenced as having offended, including those who have been banned/excluded'.

In October, human rights groups including Liberty and Amnesty International wrote to leading UK retailers urging them to quit a police-led scheme that aims to use facial recognition to tackle shoplifting. In a letter to companies including John Lewis, Tesco, Boots and M&S about the 'Pegasus' initiative, the charities said: 'Facial recognition technology notoriously misidentifies people of colour, women and LGBTQ+ people, meaning that already marginalised groups are more likely to be subject to an invasive stop by police, or at increased risk of physical surveillance, monitoring and harassment by workers in your stores.'

A government spokesperson said facial recognition has a 'sound legal basis' and had helped police catch 'a large number of serious criminals' including people wanted for murder and sexual offences. 'The police can only use facial recognition for a policing purpose, where necessary, proportionate and fair, in line with data protection and human rights laws,' they said.

ONS figures last week put shoplifting at record levels, with more than 402,000 offences in the year to September 2023, up from 304,459 the year before.

27 January 2024

Further Reading/ Useful Websites

Further Reading
The Circle – Dave Eggers
Nineteen Eighty-Four – George Orwell
Brave New World – Aldous Huxley
Girl (In Real Life) – Tamsin Winter
Survive The Modern World: How To Be Online and Also Be Happy – Issy Beech

These books are aimed at different age ranges and reading levels. Please ask your librarian for books that may be appropriate for you.

Useful websites

www.cartwrightking.co.uk

www.ceopeducation.co.uk

www.fcdo.gov.uk

www.geographical.co.uk

www.gigit.fyi

www.giveagradago.com

www.hiddenstrength.com

www.independent.co.uk

www.jakemoore.uk

www.legalchoices.org.uk

www.libertyhumanrights.org.uk

www.ncsc.gov.uk

www.pinkaurora.co.uk

www.thecritic.co.uk

www.thegraduateproject.co.uk

www.theguardian.com

Snooper's Charter (Draft Communications Data Bill)

Draft legislation that would require Internet service providers and mobile phone companies to keep records of their user's Internet search history, emails, calls and texts.

GDPR

General Data Protection Regulation is a legal framework setting guidelines for the collecting and processing of personal information from individuals who live in the European Union. It is the toughest privacy and security law in the world.

Facial recognition

Facial recognition is a method of identification using biometric software to map, analyse and confirm the identity of a face in photograph or video. It is also a powerful surveillance tool.

Article 8: Right to privacy

Article 8 of the European Convention on Human Rights states that 'Everyone has the right for his private and family life, his home and his correspondence.' There are some exceptions to this rule, however, so this means that your right to privacy can be interfered with as long as it is 'in accordance with law' and 'necessary in a democratic society'.

Big Brother

The term comes from a character in George Orwell's novel *Nineteen Eighty-Four*, from which the phrase 'Big Brother is watching you' originated. Big Brother embodied totalitarianism; a regime where the Government controls and monitors every aspect of people's lives and behaviour.

Biometric Data

Biometrics (or biometric authentication) refers to a method of uniquely identifying people. This includes methods such as fingerprints, DNA, retinal scans (eyes) and facial recognition; something that is permanent throughout a person's lifetime and doesn't change as they age. The main uses of biometric data are for the purpose of controlling access (e.g., some laptops have fingerprint scanners) or helping tackle and prevent crime.

CCTV

Closed-circuit television (CCTV) is the use of mounted video cameras which broadcast a live image to a television screen closely watched over by someone (can be recorded). CCTV is used to observe an area in an effort to reduce and prevent crime. However, the use of CCTV has triggered a debate about security versus privacy.

Glossary

Communication Data Bill

This legislation would mean that Internet service provider (ISP) and mobile phone services would be able to gather much more data about what their customers are doing. Currently, communication monitoring is limited to data such as who people send emails to and who they ring, not the actual content of the messages themselves, for 12 months. This Bill would extend it to webmail, voice calls, social media and Internet gaming. This is why it has been labelled as the 'Snooper's Charter'. It is estimated to cost approximately £1.8 billion.

Data Protection Act 2018

The Data Protection Act controls how your personal information is used by organisations, businesses or the Government. The Data Protection Act 2018 is the UK's implementation of the General Data Protection Regulation (GDPR).

Protection of Freedoms Act 2012

An act that regulates the use of biometric data, the use of surveillance and many other things. For example, this will mean schools need to get parents' consent before processing a child's biometric information and it also introduces a code of practice for surveillance camera systems. Essentially, this is to help protect people from state intrusion in their lives.

Regulation of Investigatory Powers Act 2000 (RIPA)

RIPA is the law governing the use of covert techniques, such as surveillance and investigation, by public authorities. This means that when public authorities, such as the police or government departments, need to use covert techniques to obtain private information, they do it in a way that is respectful of human rights and only when really necessary. For example, it could be used in the case of a terror alert, for the purposes of detecting crime or even for public safety.

Surveillance

The close observation and monitoring of behaviour or activities. To keep watch over a person or group. The UK has been described as a 'surveillance society' because of its large number of CCTV cameras and the national DNA database; the UK was once referred to as 'the most surveilled country' in the Western states.

Index

Book Order Details

Order No:	938160
Date:	Nov '24
Supplier:	Issues
Cost:	Part of Subscription
Barcode No:	R71629
Class No:	323.448